PRAISE FOR
These Chains Will Be Broken

"Ramzy Baroud's book of Palestinian prisoners' stories is a remarkable work. With each story, there is a roll-call of the best of humanity: courage, struggle, determination, generosity, passion, humility and, above all, defiance of injustice. Everyone, especially those of us in the West subjected to unerring propaganda, should read this searing and beautiful book. Then understand all over again that peace and justice are not possible in the world until the Palestinians are free."

—John Pilger, award-winning Australian journalist, author
and broadcaster/documentary maker

"In this must-read 'history from below,' the Palestinians who tell their stories show prison to be a microcosm of life under conditions of occupation and colonization. As the contributors convey the crushing violence of the Israeli state that imprisons them, they also demonstrate how, against all odds, Palestinians continue to engage in practices of resistance, community-building, creativity, and intellectual production; persist in their love for one another and their homeland; and remember as well as dream of a free Palestine. Read the testimonies by these men, women and children—organic intellectuals, all—in this powerful and searingly beautiful book that helps realize the promise that the chains of Zionism will be broken."

—Cynthia Franklin, Professor of English at the University
of Hawai`i and member of the USACBI Organizing Collective

"Prison is one of the most vicious tools used by oppressive regimes. One could easily say that it embodies modern-day slavery, a reality I myself have experienced first-hand. Since Israel's 1967 invasion and occupation of Palestinian territories, there have been over 750,000 Palestinians imprisoned in Israeli jails, including over 23,000 women and 25,000 children. These unjustified detentions have been perpetrated in order to punish people for their persistence and struggle to gain their freedom, realize justice, and retain their dignity. Ramzy Baroud's new book, *These Chains will be Broken,* is a powerful collection of stories of Palestinians who have not just been primary witnesses of Israeli brutality, but also shining examples of determined individuals willing to stand up for their rights, speak their conscience, and fight for their humanity. Baroud's book provides agency to those whose stories have been suppressed and marginalized for decades. He brings their voices alive with his vivid, spirited, and powerful storytelling to be heard by millions. While their oppressors try to deny their existence and humanity, Baroud brings them back and, with their memories, the plight of many thousands in Israeli jails waiting for the day they will celebrate their freedom and the liberation of their homeland. The lively, beautiful, and painful narratives recited in *These Chains will be Broken* are a must-read for anyone with a burning conscience and a determined will to see that oppression is not forgotten, freedom will be gained, and justice will ultimately prevail."

—Prof. Dr. Sami A. Al-Arian, Director and Public Affairs
Professor, Center for Islam and Global Affairs

"In this book, you will delve into the lives of men and women, read intimate stories that they have chosen to share with you, stories that may surprise you, anger you and even shock you. But they are crucial stories that must be told, read and retold. When you read this book, you will have a frame of reference that will enable you to imagine, now and always, what life in an Israeli prison is like. These are the stories of men and women who have collectively decided to never break, no matter how great the pressure and the pain."

—Khalida Jarrar, Freed Prisoner, Member of
the Palestine Legislative Council

"Unjust imprisonment is an atrocity and a desecration of international law. Therefore, it is important to understand the personal plights of people who have suffered extreme injustices that have stripped them of their freedom, their loved ones and their human rights. This book is essential in helping us develop a compassionate understanding of the plight of Palestinian prisoners and the Palestinian people. I pray for an existence where people from diverse backgrounds can live in an environment of mutual respect, peace and harmony."

—Maryum Ali, Social Worker, Public Speaker, Daughter of
Legendary American boxer and political dissident, Muhammad Ali

These Chains Will Be Broken

Palestinian Stories of Struggle and Defiance in Israeli Prisons

RAMZY BAROUD

FOREWORD
Khalida Jarrar

AFTERWORD
Richard Falk

Clarity Press, Inc.

ISBN: 978-1-949762-10-5
EBOOK ISBN: 978-1-949762-09-9

Production team:
  Abdallah Aljamal
  Romana Rubeo
  Sylvia DeMelo
  Fida Jiryis
  Yousef Aljamal

In-house editor: Diana G. Collier

Cover design: R. Jordan Santos

Cover image and extensive interior artwork by Dalia Alkayyali,
  see Table of Illustrations

Clarity Press, Inc.
2625 Piedmont Rd. NE, Ste. 56
Atlanta, GA. 30324
https://www.claritypress.com

To Razan al-Najar (1996-2018):
Martyrs don't die; they soar.

Dear Pam,

Resistane is taking a
brave moral stance against
Injustice in all of its forms.

Thank you & your
solidarity.

Ramzy Baroud
Seattle WA
2020

TABLE OF CONTENTS

ACKNOWLEDGEMENTS ix

TABLE OF ILLUSTRATIONS xiii

FOREWORD xvii
   Khalida Jarrar, Member, Palestinian
   Legislative Council

INTRODUCTION: Palestine's Organic Intellectuals 1
   Ramzy Baroud

HANAN IS "TENDERNESS" 11
   Wafa Ibrahim Samir al-Bis

GHADEER 19
   Mohammad al-Deirawi

MY BROKEN LEG: MY SOARING SPIRIT 27
   Dareen Tatour

FOR MY LITTLE BROTHER 37
   Jalal Lutfi Saqr

AVENGING SABRA AND SHATILA 45
   Kifah Sobhi 'Afifi

ME AND ISLAM 55
   Mohammad Mohammad Abu Hasira

THE GIRL WHO DID NOTHING 63
   Dima Ismail al-Wawi

DECODING THE WORLD OUTSIDE 71
   Hilal Mohammad Jaradat

LOVE BEHIND BARS 79
   Nael al-Barghouti and Iman Nafi'

HUMANITARIAN HERO 87
Mohammed Khalil al-Halabi

THE COHORT OF DEFIANCE 95
Khalida Jarrar

"I CANNOT LOSE MY HUSBAND" 105
Mohammad Adeeb al-Qiq

"THEY HELD A FUNERAL FOR ME" 115
Azmi Ahmad Mansour

THE BOY FROM HARIS 121
Ali Yasin Shamlawi

THE "BOSTA" IS AN IRON CAGE 127
Khadija Ahmad Ibrahim Khweis

LAST WORDS 133
Fouad Qasim al-Razim

MIRACULOUS BIRTH 139
Rafat Salah Mi'rif

MOHAMMAD'S WATCH 145
Bilal Khaled al-Tammam

"NO PAIN LIKE MINE" 155
Israa' Riyad Ja'abis

"I SEE YOU IN MY HEART" 163
Faris Baroud

AFTERWORD: Why International Law Matters
to Palestinian Prisoners, but Not to Israel 169
Richard Falk, former United Nations
Special Rapporteur on the Situation of
Human Rights in the Palestinian Territories

APPENDIX: Israeli Prisons 177

ACKNOWLEDGMENTS

I WOULD LIKE TO START by thanking all the women and men who shared intimate, difficult and often harrowing episodes of their lives with us. To these prisoners and their families, thank you for making this book possible. By allowing us into your lives and the lives of your loved ones—those who are still in prison or those who have passed away—you opened a window to the often unseen, unheard and unexplored trauma experienced by hundreds of thousands of Palestinians in the last few decades.

Wafa Samir al-Bis from Gaza was the first to share her story with us. The dignified and articulate way in which she communicated her painful memories made us feel that we had taken the first step in the right direction to produce this volume.

Fouad al-Razim, Mona Ja'abis, Mohammad al-Deirawi, Dima al-Wawi, Jalal Saqr, Kifah Sobhi 'Afif, Hilal Jaradat, N'imeh Shamlawi, Bilal al-Tammam, Farida Mi'rif, Azmi Mansour, Khadija Khewis, Khalil al-Halabi, Fayha' Shalash, Mohamad Abu Hasira, Iman Nafi' and Dareen Tatour, this is your book. It carries your words, voices, sentiments, poems and every other form of expression that you used to communicate this material to us. I hope that we did your powerful experiences some justice in the way we constructed, interpreted and presented your narratives.

Khalida Jarrar, a freed prisoner, educator and beloved Palestinian leader has shared her story with us, and has helped situate the book so beautifully and effectively in a proper revolutionary context by writing the Foreword as well. Thank you, Khalida. You are a role model for a generation of women and men in Palestine.

Richard Falk, Professor Emeritus of international law at Princeton University, has provided an essential legal context to this book. As the former United Nations Special Rapporteur on the Situation of Human Rights in the Palestinian Territories (2008-2014), Professor Falk helped define a legal discourse on Palestinian human rights, one that challenged all attempts at marginalizing the rights of the Palestinian people. His contribution to this book is most precious. Thank you, Richard.

I would also like to thank the production team who helped in gathering material, conducting interviews, translating and editing. Abdallah Aljamal, a brilliant journalist in Gaza, was indispensable to the process of gathering the original Arabic material. His tireless work in research, liaising with numerous individuals and conducting initial interviews helped identify the prisoners and their families whose stories are told in this book. His immaculate text, prepared in Arabic and based on the writings and interviews with many of the freed prisoners or families of prisoners, was the main source of raw material upon which this book has been written. Thank you, also, to the other researchers and journalists, Sama'a Abu Sharar and Haifa Irshaid, in Lebanon and Jordan, respectively, for helping to conduct interviews with freed Palestinian prisoners outside Palestine.

A special thank you to Romana Rubeo, who has assisted in the process of producing this book from its inception to the final stages of editing and presenting the text. Her input and active participation in preparing and finalizing all content have made this book possible. Romana, your vital assistance in this project is most appreciated. Thank you.

Yousef Aljamal, a young Palestinian scholar, translator and writer, helped in facilitating much of the material contained in this book. Yousef also assisted in research and offered most valuable advice throughout the writing process. I thank him for his continued assistance and support.

A special thank you to the wonderful proofreading and editing team consisting of Sylvia DeMelo, Fida Jiryis and Suzanne Baroud. Their immaculate editing, their invaluable suggestions regarding the text and their patience are responsible for producing the quality content presented in this volume. I thank them all very much for their excellent work and for being so generous with their time. Moreover, Fida Jiryis has helped in preparing, writing and editing the text of Azmi Mansour's story: "They held a funeral for me."

Lena Khalaf Tuffaha translated two important passages in the book, a poem by freed prisoner Dareen Tatour and a song by the late Ria Baroud, which helped give both stories more substance and depth. Thank you, Lena, for all of your help.

A special thank you to the talented artist, Dalia Al Kayyali, for producing the original art to be used as a cover for this book. Thank you also to the artists Deb Van Poolen, Marguerite Debaie and Tashi Farmilo-Marouf.

Thank you to Professor Cynthia Franklin, Claude Zurback, Joe Catron, Professor J. Kēhaulani Kauanui, M. Healani Sonoda-Pale, Roger Fowler, Professor Sami Al-Arian, Michel Tellone, veteran journalist Tim Llewellyn, journalist Salwa Amore, and Maryum Ali, a community leader and daughter of the legendary American boxer and political dissident, Muhammad Ali.

Keeping in mind that John Pilger has had a profound influence on my writing and journalistic work, his endorsement of this book was particularity special and heartwarming. Thank you, John, for your support and for all the critical work that you continue to produce.

Thank you, Diana G. Collier and Clarity Press, for taking on this project, for creating a platform for these powerful, yet often unheard Palestinian voices, and for all the quality and courageous work that you publish.

Last but not least, thank you to my ever patient, loving and supportive children, Zarefah, Iman and Sammy. You remain my true inspiration in this life.

—Ramzy Baroud

TABLE OF ILLUSTRATIONS

1   Dalia Alkayyali (b. 1976), *Soul Rebellion 1* (2014)
    Ink on mixed media paper, 8.3 x 11.7 in. xvi

2   Dalia Alkayyali, *The Key* (2015)
    Acrylic on canvas, 20 x 40 in. xxii

3   Dalia Alkayyali, *Soul Rebellion 2* (2014)
    Ink on mixed media paper, 8.3 x 11.7 in. 10

4   Dalia Alkayyali, *Soul Rebellion 3* (2014)
    Ink on mixed media paper, 8.3 x 11.7 in. 18

5   Dalia Alkayyali, *Untitled,*
    Inspired by Mahmoud Darwish poem (2018)
    Ink on mixed media paper, 11.69 x 16.53 in. 26

6. Dareen Tatour (b. 1982)..32

7   Dalia Alkayyali, *I Came from There* (2017)
    Acrylic on canvas, 48 x 48 in. 36

8   Dalia Alkayyali, *Freedom* (2013)
    Ink on mixed media paper, 8.3 x 11.7 in. 44

9   Dalia Alkayyali, *Peace in the City,* Part 2 (2018)
    Mixed media, 36 x 48 in..54

10 Dalia Alkayyali, *Soul Rebellion 4* (2014), Inspired
    by Taqfiq Zayyad poem, "Here We Shall Stay"
    Ink on mixed media paper, 8.3 x 11.7 in. 62

11 Dalia Alkayyali, *Soul Rebellion 5* (2014), Inspired
    by Taqfiq Zayyad poem, "Here We Shall Stay"
    Ink on mixed media paper, 8.3 x 11.7 in. 70

12 Dalia Alkayyali, *Love in Palestinian Way* (2015)
    Copic marker on mixed media paper,
    11.69 x 16.53 in. 78

13 Dalia Alkayyali, *Heaven,* Part 3 (2014)
    Mixed media (paper, acrylic and ink)
    on canvas, 31 x 31 in. 86

14 Dalia Alkayyali, *Untitled,*
    In Memory of Mahmoud Darwish (2014)
    Acrylic on canvas, 20 x 24 in. 94

15 Dalia Alkayyali, *The Pigeons Fly,*
    Inspired by Mahmoud Darwish poem (2013)
    Oil on canvas, 36 x 48 in. 102

16 Dalia Alkayyali, *Freedom* (2013)
    Ink on mixed media paper, 8.3 x 11.7 in. 114

17 Dalia Alkayyali, *Alquds* (2011)
    Copic marker on mixed media paper,
    8.3 x 11.7 in. 120

18 Dalia Alkayyali, *Soul Rebellion 6* (2014)
    Ink on mixed media paper, 8.3 x 11.7 in. 126

19 Dalia Alkayyali, *Soul Rebellion 7* (2014)
    Ink on mixed media paper, 8.3 x 11.7 in. 132

20 Dalia Alkayyali, *To My Mother* (2014)
    Oil on canvas, 36 x 48 in. 138

21 Dalia Alkayyali, *Heaven,* Part 2 (2014)
    Mixed media (paper, acrylic and ink) on
    canvas, 31 x 31 in. 144

22 Dalia Alkayyali, *Yafa* (2011)
    Copic marker on mixed media paper,
    18 x 24 in. 154

23 Dalia Alkayyali, *Peace in the City,* Part 5 (2018)
    Mixed media, 36 x 48 in...162

24 Dalia Alkayyali, *Yafa* (2011)
    Copic marker on mixed media paper,
    18 x 24 in..168

25 Romana Rubeo, *Map of Prisons*..............................176

1

FOREWORD

PRISON is not just a place made of high walls, barbed wire and small, suffocating cells with heavy iron doors. It is not just a place that is defined by the clanking sound of metal; indeed, the screeching or slamming of metal is the most common sound you will hear in prisons, whenever heavy doors are shut, when heavy beds or cupboards are moved, when handcuffs are locked in position or loosened. Even the bosta—the notorious vehicles that transport prisoners from one prison facility to another—are metal beasts, their interior, their exterior, even their doors and built-in shackles.

No, prison is more than all of this. It is also stories of real people, daily suffering and struggles against the prison guards and administration. Prison is a moral position that must be made daily, and can never be put behind you.

Prison is comrades—sisters and brothers who, with time, grow closer to you than your own family. It is common agony, pain, sadness and, despite everything, also joy at times.

In prison, we challenge the abusive prison guard together, with the same will and determination to break him so that he does not break us. This struggle is unending and is manifested in every possible form, from the simple act of refusing our meals, to confining ourselves to our rooms, to the most physically and physiologically strenuous of all efforts, the open hunger strike. These are but some of the tools which Palestinian prisoners use to fight for, and earn, their very basic rights and to preserve some of their dignity.

Prison is the art of exploring possibilities; it is a school that trains you to solve daily challenges using the simplest and most creative means, whether it be food preparation, mending old clothes or finding common ground so that we may all endure and survive together.

In prison, we must become aware of time, because if we do not, it will stand still. So, we do everything we can to fight the routine, to take every opportunity to celebrate and to commemorate every important occasion in our lives, personal or collective.

I am honored to be part of this book, sharing my own story and writing this preface. In this book, you will delve into the lives of men and women, read intimate stories that they have chosen to share with you, stories that may surprise you, anger you and even shock you. But they are crucial stories that must be told, read and retold.

The stories in this book are not written to shock you, but rather to illustrate even a small part of the daily reality endured by thousands of men and women, who are still confined within high walls, barbed wire and metal doors. When you read this book, you will have a frame of reference that will enable you to imagine, now and always, what life in an Israeli prison is like.

And every story, whether included in this book or not, is not a fleeting experience that only concerns the person who has lived it, but an event that shakes to the very core the prisoner, her comrades, her family and her entire community. Each story represents a creative interpretation of a life lived, despite all the hardship, by a person whose heart beats with the love of her homeland and the longing for her precious freedom. Each individual narrative is also a defining moment, a conflict between the will of the prison guard and all that he represents, and the will of the prisoners and what they represent as a collective, capable, when united, of overcoming incredible odds.

In actuality, these are not just prison stories. For Palestinians, the prison is a microcosm of the much larger struggle of a people who refuse to be enslaved on their own land, and who are determined to regain their freedom, with the same will and vigor carried by all triumphant, once-colonized nations.

The suffering and the human rights violations experienced by Palestinian prisoners, which run contrary to international and humanitarian law, are only one side of the prison story. The other side can only be truly understood and conveyed by those who have lived these harrowing experiences. This book will allow you to live part of that experience by briefly touching the inspiring human trajectory of Palestinian men and women who have subsisted through defining moments, with all of their painful details and challenges.

Here, you can imagine what it feels like to lose a loving mother while being confined to a small cell, how to deal with a broken leg, to be left without family visitation for years at a time, to be denied your right to education and to cope with the death of a comrade. While you will learn of the numerous acts of physical torture, psychological torment and prolonged isolation, you will also discover the power of the human will, when men and women decide to fight back, to reclaim their natural rights and to embrace their humanity.

Indeed, these are the stories of men and women who have collectively decided to never break, no matter how great the pressure and the pain.

I would like to conclude by saluting every female and every male prisoner who are eagerly awaiting the moment of their freedom and the freedom of their people. I salute those whose stories are written in this book and I thank them for allowing us a window into an intimate, painful chapter of their lives. As for those whose stories were not conveyed here, simply because there are thousands upon thousands of personal narratives left untold, you are always in our hearts and minds.

Dear reader, please play your part, by listening to and conveying the stories of Palestinians, whether those who are captive in Israeli prisons or those suffocated under Israeli occupation. Carry and communicate their message to the world so that, someday, the walls of every prison may come tumbling down, ushering in the age of Palestinian freedom.

—Khalida Jarrar, Freed Prisoner and
Member of the Palestine Legislative Council

2

INTRODUCTION

PALESTINE'S ORGANIC INTELLECTUALS

"FOR MY OPINIONS," wrote Italian intellectual Antonio Gramsci, *"I am willing to lose my life, not only to stay in prison. And this is why I am calm and at peace with myself."*[1] Gramsci spent 11 years in prison during the fascist reign over Italy, a brutal regime that crushed every form of political dissent between 1922 and 1943. He died only six days after he was released.

Gramsci's revolutionary life and untimely death at the age of 46 reflected his own definition of the "organic intellectual," someone who is not a mere "mover of feelings and passions" but an "active participant in practical life, as constructor and organizer—a 'permanent persuader,' not just a simple orator."[2]

This definition qualifies all men and women to be intellectuals, as per Gramsci's thinking, even if they do not possess that function in society, simply because "there is no human activity from which every form of intellectual participation can be excluded," particularly those activities that are guided by "a conscious line of moral conduct."[3]

---

1 Antonio Gramsci, *Lettere dal carcere* (Torino, Einaudi, 1971).
2 Antonio Gramsci, *Gli intellettuali e l'organizzazione della cultura,* edited by F. Platone (Torino, Nuovo Universale Einaudi).
3 Antonio Gramsci, ibid.

All the people whose stories are being told in this book, every single one of them, possess a claim to true, organic intellect. They all fought for an idea, an opinion, were—and are—willing to lose their lives to defend these ideas. In the case of Faris Baroud ("I See You in My Heart"), and many other Palestinian prisoners, they have, indeed, done so.

These are the stories of Palestine's true intellectuals, women and men, mothers and fathers, children and teens, teachers, fighters and human rights advocates, united by a single motive that transcends region, religion and ideology: resistance, that is, taking a brave moral stance against injustice in all of its forms.

It would be utterly unfair to box Palestinian prisoners into convenient categories of victims or terrorists, because both classifications render an entire nation either victim or terrorist, a notion that does not reflect the true nature of the decades-long Palestinian struggle against colonialism, military occupation and the entrenched Israeli apartheid.

According to United Nations[4] and Palestinian sources,[5] between 750,000 and 800,000 Palestinians have been imprisoned since the Israeli occupation of East Jerusalem, the West Bank and the Gaza Strip in June 1967. They include 23,000 women and 25,000 children. Currently, there are 5,250 Palestinian political prisoners in Israel, a number that is constantly growing, not only because Israel insists on maintaining its military occupation, but

---

4 "United Nations Special Rapporteur on the Situation of Human Rights in the Palestinian Territories Occupied since 1967 Raises Alarm over Palestinian Prisoners in Hunger Strike," United Nations, accessed July 29, 2019, <https://unispal.un.org/UNISPAL.NSF/0/EF6E79DCD608D68385257A3E006838A9>.

5 "Over 800,000 Palestinians Imprisoned by Israel since 1967, Says Erekat," Haaretz, April 17, 2014, <https://www.haaretz.com/.premium-800-000-palestinians-jailed-since-67-1.5245393>.

also because Palestinians insist on their right to resist it. Expectedly, Israel dubs any form of Palestinian resistance an act of "terrorism," a misleading depiction of the reality of Palestinian political dissent which ultimately aims at their dehumanization, and thus justifying the subjugation of an entire nation. But Palestinians are not passive victims, either.

"In the end, we did more than fashion hope out of despair," wrote Khalida Jarrar, a Palestinian leader and prisoner, in her story, "The Cohort of Defiance":

> *We also evolved in our narrative, in the way we perceive ourselves, the prison and the prison guards. We defeated any lingering sense of inferiority and turned the walls of prison into an opportunity. When I saw the beautiful smiles on the faces of my students who completed their high school education in prison, I felt that my mission has been accomplished.*[6]

Jarrar, who also wrote the Foreword to this book, is Gramsci's true organic intellectual in its most ideal manifestation. She has been more than a "mover of feelings and passions," and has defiantly and tirelessly challenged her tormentors, educated a generation of women who were denied such opportunities in prison, and has never deviated from her strong, revolutionary discourse. It is no surprise that she was imprisoned repeatedly by Israel. Each time, she emerged stronger, more defiant and determined.

Dima al-Wawi is Khalida Jarrar in the making. At the age of 12, she was arrested, tried and imprisoned on the basis of the ever-convenient charges of attempting to stab a fully-

---

6 See chapter, "The Cohort of Defiance," p. 95.

armed Israeli settler, near the settlement of Karmei Tzur, which was built illegally on Palestinian land that belongs to her town of Halhul, north of Al-Khalil (Hebron).

"After I was released I returned to the Halhul Martyrs School," she wrote:

> *It was wonderful to be back, and I cannot wait to finish my education and become a journalist, carrying the message of the prisoners and their suffering to the world. I want to show the world how the children of Palestine are mistreated every day by the occupation.*[7]

In prison, many Palestinian female prisoners protected young Dima, serving the role of mother and older sister, in itself an act of solidarity that defines Palestinian society. Israa Ja'abis is one of these prisoners who assumed the role of family; her story inside prison is conveyed through her sister, Mona.[8]

"The harshness of the occupier scarred her face and body, amputated her fingers and is relentlessly trying to break her spirit," wrote Mona. The fact that Israa embraced Dima during her short stay in the Ofer Prison is proof that the young mother's spirit was never broken, although severe burns have covered most of her body.

Whether Khalida, Dima, Israa, Ali, Dareen, Faris and all others have met in prison, in court or anywhere else, matters little. Their lives are connected at their very core. The struggle is one and the same. Their stories are elaborations on the same narrative, that of engaged resisters, organic

---

7 See chapter, "The Girl Who Did Nothing," p. 63.
8 See chapter, "'No Pain Like Mine,'" p. 155.

intellectuals who are serving a higher cause than their own freedom: the freedom of their people.

And because Palestinian resistance is a collective experience, the writing of this book has also been a collective effort. It is our attempt to reclaim the narrative of our people, to liberate it from the suffocating confines of political, media and academic discourse and take it into the heart of the resistance. *These Chains Will Be Broken* is a collection of the stories of Palestinian resisters, either conveyed by them, or through close family members, in an intimate setting that is free from the typical representation and misrepresentation of Palestine and her people. Here, the prisoners will not be defending themselves as if in an Israeli military court, or trying to directly address media reporting about their presumed "guilt." Nor will the issue of violent vs. non-violent resistance be dealt with. Such a "debate" may satisfy the theoretical preoccupations of western audiences in far-away academic circles, but none of these prisoners—whether accused of killing Israeli soldiers or of writing a poem—have sought to classify their muqawama—resistance—in any way.

The stories in this book were written directly or conveyed in person, through interviews or audio recordings, by those who have lived them. The initial research questions that prisoners or their families were asked to address sought to elicit an understanding of the prison experience and its impact on the individual, the family and the community. The end result provided here expresses the individually unique experience of each prisoner, while highlighting a recurring theme—a thread in the narrative that represents the collective story of Palestinian resistance.

While conducting interviews related to the book with several freed Palestinian prisoners in Istanbul, Turkey in April 2019, I was astonished by the clarity of their political discourse. Of the three prisoners we interviewed, one was associated with the political movement Fatah, another with Hamas, and a third with Islamic Jihad. Despite the seemingly great ideological divides among the three groups, I was struck by the degree of unity and cohesion in their individual narratives when it came to the subject of resistance, whether in or outside prison. As the book demonstrates, muqawama is the common denominator among all prisoners; in fact, among all Palestinians.

The above truth explains, in part, why we have chosen this form of narrative to tell the story of Palestinian prisoners and, by extension, the story of Palestinian resistance as a whole. As in all my previous books, I am compelled by this imperative to relocate the centrality of the Palestine narrative from an Israeli perspective to a Palestinian one, especially one that overlooks the typical, elitist angle and focuses, instead, on retelling the story from the viewpoint of ordinary, poor, underprivileged and working-class Palestinians.

Undoubtedly, however, this work is not mine alone. I and those who have dedicated to putting this book together, are mere conveyors of ideas, notions and the intelligence of Palestine's true organic intellectuals, even if they are not accorded such a role in society. On the other hand, these are also our stories, for all the Palestinian contributors who helped facilitate and assemble the content of this book have also experienced Israeli imprisonment in various forms. I lived in a Gaza refugee camp for much of my life and was held, along with thousands of my fellow refugees, under protracted military curfews, some lasting months at a time. It is this "positionality" that allowed me, together with other Palestinian researchers, to be able to relate to the text in an entirely different way. This is not a detached journalistic or academic text. It is our own collective story, as well.

Indeed, the "prison" in this book is a metaphor for the collective Palestinian prison experience. All Palestinians are prisoners—those held in besieged Gaza or those trapped behind walls, fences and checkpoints in the West Bank. All experience some manifestation of prison every day of their lives. Even those trapped in their seemingly endless exiles, unable to reunite with their families or visit their Palestinian homes, are also enduring that prison experience in one way or another.

One would dare to claim that Israelis, too, are prisoners, though of a different kind. *"A man who takes away another man's freedom is a prisoner of hatred, he is locked behind the bars of prejudice and narrow-mindedness,"* wrote the late iconic anti-Apartheid hero and long-time prisoner, Nelson Mandela. *"The oppressed and the oppressor alike are robbed of their humanity."*[9]

I believe that this book needed to be written. This stems from my insistence that only "people's history" or "history from below"[10] is capable of unearthing and fairly conveying reality in the most egalitarian and democratic way. Specifically, people's history directly defies two, dominant narratives concerning Palestine: the elitist rationalization of Palestinian political reality (which sees history as an outcome of the workings of an individual or a faction/group), and the reductionist approach to any subject concerning Palestinians, a discourse that teeters between the extremist view, which denies their very existence, and that which presents their struggle and national aspirations as a

---

9 Nelson Mandela, *A Long Walk to Freedom* (Boston, Little Brown & Co., 1994).

10 "History from Below is a major trend in the twentieth century historiography that marks a reaction against the traditional histories almost exclusively concerned with the socio-political and religious elites. 'Grassroots history,' 'history seen from below,' 'history of the common people,' 'people's history,' and 'history of everyday life' are some of the terms alternatively used for it." "What Is History from Below?" Scribd, accessed July 28, 2019, <https://www.scribd.com/document/215659476/What-is-History-From-Below>.

"problem" to be quickly—if not haphazardly—remedied.

The story of Palestine cannot be truly appreciated through the understanding of the counter-claims on this precious piece of land: those made by the original inhabitants of Palestine, the Palestinian people, and those by mostly European colonialists, who began arriving in Palestine in the late 19th century. The Palestinian story is also that of emotions, of resistance and sacrifice, of defiance and sumoud, steadfastness. Though it is a Palestinian story, it is also the story of every nation that has fought against injustice, regardless of when and how it expressed itself.

Antonio Gramsci could have easily been a Palestinian prisoner, as Faris Baroud could have been an Italian partisan, fighting fascism. The former wrote to his mother from prison; the latter never received his mother's letters to him.

"Dearest mum," wrote Gramsci:

> *I would love to hug you tight to show you how much I love you and to relieve some of the pain that I caused you, but I couldn't do otherwise. That's life, it is very hard, and sometimes children must deeply hurt their own mother, to preserve their honor and their dignity as human beings.[11]*

"Oh, how I cried for you, Faris," wrote Ria Baroud:

> *My eyes can only tell day from night, but nothing else. But thanks to God, thanks to God, I am content with my fate, for this is what Allah has decided for me. It is you that I am concerned about. So, I pray all day, every*

---

11 Antonio Gramsci, *supra.*

day. I make supplications to God so that you come back, and that I may choose your bride for you. We will throw a big party and all the neighbors and friends, all the Barouds and all the freed prisoners and their families will come and celebrate with us.[12]

Antonio Gramsci died on April 27, 1937 from a cerebral hemorrhage, only six days after he was released.

Faris Baroud died on February 6, 2019, from a kidney disease, in Nafha Prison in the Naqab Desert.

They were both organic intellectuals of the highest caliber.

—*Ramzy Baroud*

---

12 See chapter, "'I See You in My Heart,'" p. 163.

3

HANAN IS "TENDERNESS"

Wafa Ibrahim Samir al-Bis

WHEN Wafa al-Bis was arrested on May 20, 2005, she was wearing an explosive belt. The 21-year-old was on a mission to blow herself up among Israeli soldiers stationed at the Beit Hanoun checkpoint. This checkpoint, known as "Eretz," separates occupied Gaza from Israel. Instead of succeeding in her mission, she was captured, detained, and later sentenced to 12 years in prison.

At 17, Wafa had her entire life ahead of her when she saw television footage of the Gazan child, Mohammed al-Durra, being shot and killed by Israeli troops as he clung to his father, Jamal, who tried in vain to shield his son from the hail of bullets. It was September 2000. Mohammed was killed at the scene and his father was critically injured. The event symbolized the horrors witnessed by Palestinians during the Second Palestinian Intifada, a popular uprising that lasted for approximately five years (2000-2005).

In preparation for the "martyrdom attack,"[13] Wafa wrote a letter that served as a last will and testament, explaining that she felt that such an act was the only way she

---

13 "Martyrdom attack" is the translation from Arabic of "a'amaliyya istishhadiyya," or what is often referred to as a suicide bombing.

could avenge the young boy's cold-blooded murder. This was not a spontaneous decision; Wafa rigorously trained with a Gaza-based group for nearly nine months. Her attempt was thwarted and the man who trained her was killed by the Israeli army, three months after Wafa's arrest.

Of the total duration of her sentence, she spent nearly six and a half years in prison, where she was subjected to severe torture and two years in solitary confinement. Wafa was released on October 18, 2011, alongside hundreds of Palestinians in a prisoner exchange between the Hamas movement and the Israeli government. Months later, she married a fellow refugee, and, together, they have two little boys, Hasan and Bara.' The family now lives in Gaza's "Prisoners' City."[14] Wafa's fight has never ceased, but she struggles to endure the mental and physical scars of her imprisonment, the harsh life under siege in Gaza and an unrelenting fear for the future of her children.

Wafa's parents are refugees from Hamameh, a small village destroyed during the Zionist ethnic cleansing of Palestine in 1947–48, an event known to Palestinians as the "Nakba,"[15] or catastrophe. They patiently wait to return to

---

14 Prisoners' City is a specially-designated neighborhood built in March 2015, southwest of Gaza City, to accommodate hundreds of freed Palestinian prisoners and their families. "Ghazza: Al-Hasayneh wa al-Ammadi Yudashinan Mashrou' Madinet Al-Shaik Hamad Lilasra al Muhararin," Al Ayyam, accessed August 3, 2019, <http://www.al-ayyam.ps/ar_page.php?id=eecdca6y250404006Yeecdca6>.

15 "The Palestinian 'Nakba' ('catastrophe' in Arabic) refers to the mass expulsion of Palestinian Arabs from British Mandate Palestine during Israel's creation (1947-49). The Nakba was not an unintended result of war. It was a deliberate and systematic act necessary for the creation of a Jewish majority state in historic Palestine, which was overwhelmingly Arab prior to 1948. Internally, Zionist Jewish leaders used the euphemism 'transfer' when discussing plans for what today would be called ethnic cleansing." "Quick Facts, the Palestinian Nakba," Institute for Middle East Understanding, accessed August 4, 2019, <https://imeu.org/article/quick-facts-the-palestinian-nakba>.

their historic homeland and are temporarily living in the Jabaliya refugee camp in Gaza.

———————◆———————

SHE WAS A GIFT FROM GOD. I named her Hanan, which means "tenderness," after my favorite sister and because I was alone. It had been years since I felt the love of a mother, a father, a sister or a brother. She became my only family during my solitary confinement at the Ramleh prison.[16]

I found in Hanan a kind of humanity that I did not experience since I was thrown into my underground Israeli dungeon. She just wandered into the prison yard, unnoticed. I lured her in with the crumbs of whatever terrible food my prison guards would slide under my door. I entrusted her with my most intimate feelings, and she, despite her gaunt, shrunken body, saved me from the eternal darkness of my isolation, which lasted for two years.

My story with Hanan started as soon as an Israeli military court sentenced me to two years in solitary confinement. This order came after I was convicted of attacking a female Israeli prison guard with a sharp object. That guard had tormented me for so long, mocking me and calling me "terrorist" at every turn. One day, she exclaimed with a laugh: "We have just killed the terrorist who recruited you." She leaned in close to the bars of my cell and, without hesitation, I jumped up and slashed her face.

Before solitary, I was placed among inmates with criminal records. They were Israelis and they, too, tried to break me, but when I was sentenced with an additional court order, I was placed in "Cell No. 9," all alone. There, my hardship grew tenfold. My physical and psychological torture intensified, but I was determined to stay strong.

---

16 See Appendix.

My will remained unbending, with strong faith in God and constant praying and reading of the Holy Quran. At times, I resorted to drawing. I am not an artist, but translating my feelings onto paper helped me channel my fear and anxiety.

I met Hanan during "al-foura,"[17] the short recess during which I was allowed to leave my cell for very brief periods of time. The courtyard was a small concrete floor with high walls, as if designed to look like a cage. My entrapment was unbearable—until I met Hanan. Her hazel eyes were so beautiful and innocent. In them, I saw hope in a place filled with despair.

My darling Hanan was very, very beautiful. I adopted her. I looked after her, groomed her and shared my food with her. When the prison administration would cut down the rations to punish me, I would give it all to Hanan, because the love and warmth I received from her far exceeded whatever love I could have given her. I used to talk to her for hours as a close friend. I know that she felt deep sadness for my adversity and truly felt my suffering. And whenever she winced, I felt that she was saying: "Yes, I hear you and I feel your pain."

My cell was underground. At first, I visited with Hanan in the prison's concrete courtyard. I built her a little house using discarded cardboard. I snuck food out of my cell whenever I went on al-foura, and would place it inside her house. That is how I was able to familiarize her with her new place. When our friendship became stronger, she would come looking for me in my cell. I would save her the only piece of chicken I received with my meal every Friday, because Hanan liked meat. She would sense my presence at the door of my cell and come running. When she drew closer, I would stick my hand out of the little opening of

---

17 'Foura' is the yard time granted to prisoners.

my cell door to caress her. I would peer out of the door and look into her eyes and talk to her for a long time. I told her many a time that I was lonely, and that the walls of my cell were closing in on me. I told her that I was a prisoner with so much pain and that no one could understand my suffering. I told her how much I missed visits from my family, who were forbidden from seeing me for years. I told her how I was unjustly treated and that this was not my place in this world. She would look at me and hang on every word as if she understood my anguish.

One day, I asked the prison guard for a cup of tea, as I was denied having access to any food or drink in my cell. I was surprised when she agreed. She asked me to extend my hand from the little trap door to fetch the cup; when I did, she poured boiling water all over my hand, leaving me with third degree burns that continue to cause me tremendous pain to this day. I still hope that, someday, someone will help me treat my unhealed wounds. On that day, I screamed in pain for hours and no one came to my rescue, except for Hanan. She ran to my door and she wept. We cried together for a long time.

Sometime later, I realized Hanan was pregnant. I reinforced her cardboard home and covered the floor with one of the two dresses that I was allowed to keep in my cell. I used my favorite white dress. I cut it into small pieces and lined the floor with it; then I moved the whole box behind the portable toilet in the courtyard for extra safety. When she finally gave birth, I increased the portions of food and water for her and her kittens.

But the guards found out. They told me: "This is unacceptable and disgusting." I wept in front of them. I cried: "Please don't take my friend away. Please don't separate us."

I felt that they thoroughly enjoyed seeing me in this desperate condition. To further my torment, they poisoned

Hanan and her babies. I watched the little kittens cling to their mom's side as they reeled in pain; I sat beside them, sobbing and imploring God for mercy. The guards laughed and stomped on them as they screamed in agony. A large guard placed his heavy boot on Hanan's face and crushed it. To this day, I still hear their voices. I am constantly visited by the horrific images of the pool of blood and the bodies of my best friend and her babies scattered around the prison yard. Hanan was the only hope that kept me strong, and the Israelis crushed it without mercy.

After the death of Hanan and her little ones, I launched an open hunger strike. I did not have any demands. It was the only human thing I could do to rebel against their inhumanity. Israelis are so blinded by hate to the point that their hearts have grown so callous. What had Hanan done to deserve such suffering? Her only crime is that she had given a ray of hope to a lonely prisoner longing for her freedom.

Hanan will live in my heart for as long as I breathe.

—Wafa Ibrahim Samir al-Bis

4

GHADEER

Mohammad al-Deirawi and Majdi Hammad

MOHAMMAD Ibrahim Ali al-Deirawi was born on January 30, 1978 in Nuseirat refugee camp in the Gaza Strip. His family is originally from Bir Al-Saba,'[18] an ethnically cleansed Palestinian town located in the southern Naqab desert. Mohammad was arrested by the Israeli army at a military checkpoint in central Gaza on March 1, 2001. He was sentenced to 30 years in prison for his role in the armed Palestinian resistance, and was freed on October 18, 2011 in a prisoner exchange between the Palestinian resistance and Israel.

Mohammad's interrogation commenced as soon as he arrived at the Central Askalan (Ashkelon)[19] Prison in southern Israel, where he experienced physical and psychological torture for nearly two and a half months. He was handed his sentence by an Israeli military court on March 20, 2003.

As soon as he was released from the Nafha Prison[20], 100 kilometers north of Bir Al-Saba,' he married Ghadeer,

---

18 The Palestinian village of Bir Al-Saba' was ethnically cleansed in 1948. Palestine Remembered, accessed August 3, 2019, <https://www.palestineremembered.com/Beersheba/Beersheba/index.html>.

19 See Appendix.

20 See Appendix.

the beautiful and only daughter of his prison-mate, Majdi Hammad. Ghadeer and Mohammad have two children.

Majdi Hammad was born on March 20, 1965 in the Jabaliya refugee camp, the most crowded and dilapidated of all of Gaza's refugee camps, and the birthplace of the First Palestinian Intifada, the popular uprising of 1987. Hammad's family originated from the ethnically cleansed village of Barbara, in southern Palestine.

Majdi was the youngest of two brothers and one sister, Fathi, Akram and Fayza. Majdi was raised mostly by his mother, Farida, known for her strong religious principles, strong character and leadership in the community.

Majdi was arrested several times, the last and longest of his prison terms being in 1991. Then, he was sentenced to 624 years in prison[21] for his leadership role in the armed resistance and, particularly, in the Qassam Brigades, the military wing of the Hamas organization. When he was arrested and imprisoned, his wife, Nahla, was still pregnant with their daughter, Ghadeer.

Majdi was released alongside Mohammad and hundreds of other prisoners in October 2011, but died soon after, on March 18, 2014, from heart disease that was left untreated for years while in Israeli prisons.

Ghadeer means small stream.

---

21   According to the Palestinian Centre for Palestinian Prisoners' Studies, life sentence "is a 99-year-prison-term that the Israeli occupation imposes on Palestinian prisoners who are accused of killing Israeli settlers or soldiers. It is also imposed on Palestinians accused of planning or directing resistance actions that led to the death of Israelis." "500 Palestinian Prisoners Serving Life Terms in Israel Jails," *Middle East Monitor,* November 16, 2017, <https://www.middleeastmonitor.com/20171116-500-palestinian-prisoners-serving-life-terms-in-israel-jails/>.

I HAVE NEVER IMAGINED THAT GHADEER COULD EVER BE MY WIFE. She was a teenage girl when I first saw her, as she accompanied her mother to the Nafha Prison to visit her father, Majdi Hamad. That was in 2002. Her dad is one of the toughest men you will ever meet, solid as a rock against his enemies, but so gentle and kind to his comrades.

I was in solitary confinement when I first met him. I saw him through the small flap door of my cell. He was being dragged into his cell in the underground dungeon of Nafha by a number of armed guards. They were hitting and kicking him everywhere and, despite his shackles, he fought back like the lion he was. His face was covered in blood. I did not know what to think of him at the time.

Majdi looked familiar, although I did not recognize him immediately. In fact, at the time, I thought he could have been in prison for one criminal offense or another, and sentenced to isolation for violent behavior against other criminals. But, later that evening, I heard him make the call for prayer. His voice was shaken and tired, but still confident and warm. "Allahu Akbar, Allahu Akbar"—"God is Great, God is Great" —he announced the evening prayer. I stood up, washed and prayed in my cell. For days after that, I kept hearing his voice reading Quranic verses from memory. It was uplifting to hear a familiar voice, to be reminded that everything happens for a reason, and that, in the end, it will all make sense, since every trial and challenge in this life is the will of God.

Luckily for me, Majdi's cell was adjacent to mine. A few days after his arrival, I gathered my courage, drew as close as I could to the shared wall and asked him: "What is your name and why are you here?" He replied: "What is yours and why are you here?"

I told him. "I am Mohammed al-Deirawi and I am from Gaza, and I am imprisoned for joining the armed resistance." He said that he, too, was from Gaza and that he was imprisoned for being a member of the resistance. But it was only when he said his name that I knew that he was no ordinary fighter. Majdi was a legend in Gaza for years, since he had formed the first martyrs' underground cell in the late 1980s, then become one of the leaders of the Qassam Brigades in the early '90s. He was sentenced to hundreds of years in prison, but he never gave up hope that he would, one day, be free. Despite the horrific physical torture he endured, he admitted to nothing. He did not concede a single name or any useful information, thus giving other fighters the chance to take necessary measures to avoid arrest or assassination.

As for myself, I spent nearly 11 years in prison, nine of them in the same section in Nafha with Majdi. Over the years, he grew from being a friend to an older brother, even a father figure to me. I loved him dearly. If it were not for Majdi, I do not know how I would have coped with my life in my underground dungeon.

Before I was brought to Nafha, I endured several long bouts of torture, each extending for 55 hours at a time. They had me stand blindfolded in the same position for 12 hours at a time. They placed me in a refrigerator-like room and kept lowering the temperature until I thought I was going to die from cold. They took shifts beating me. They tied me to an intentionally unstable chair for many hours. They placed a filthy bag on my head for long hours, leaving me gasping for breath, thinking that I would suffocate at any moment.

I was 23 at the time of my arrest. True, I was young, but I was mentally prepared for any eventuality. I had seen enough pain and suffering in my life that would have prepared me for a lot worse. I lost nearly 20 kilograms (approximately 45 pounds) during the initial torture stage, which lasted for 71 days, straight. Not only did they fail to break me; I reached a point where I simply decided not to acknowledge the existence of my interrogators. I told the officers who questioned me under constant duress: "I don't see you." They were baffled and kept yelling in my face to answer their questions, but I kept repeating: "I don't see you." All of their beating could not make me stop.

My interrogation commenced the day I was detained, on March 1, 2001. After that, I spent two years waiting for the verdict, which was handed down by an Israeli military court on March 20, 2003. I was sentenced to 30 years in prison. After announcing his decision, the judge asked me: "Do you wish to apologize for what you have done?"

"I have nothing to apologize for," I replied, with my head held high. "I will never apologize for resisting the occupation, defending my people, fighting for my stolen rights. But you need to apologize, and those who demolish homes while their owners are still inside are the ones who must apologize. Those who kill children, occupy land and commit crimes against unarmed, innocent people, are the ones who need to apologize." He did not like my answer and shouted at me to stop, but I would not.

I spent most of my time in prison in Nafha and much of it in isolation. Most of those who were with me in the same section were from Gaza. There were about 30 of us. As soon as Majdi joined us, he became our leader and protector. He helped organize our efforts, allowing us to speak with one voice. He was funny when he needed to be, and tough when the situation called for it. He was a true leader.

Prisoners from Gaza received their visitations on the same day. It was then that I met Majdi's family. When Majdi was first detained, his wife was still pregnant with Ghadeer, their firstborn and only child at the time. He watched her grow up slowly from behind thick glass, while handcuffed to a wall, unable to hold or kiss her. He spoke so much about Ghadeer, of the life he wished for her. He said that he would hold on just to be united with her some day. Majdi always wished to have a big family. It reminded him of life in Palestine before the entire Hammad clan was ethnically cleansed from their village, Barbara. Life was good back then, for all of our people, and Majdi was determined to someday return to his original village.

In the last few years of his stay at Nafha, Majdi was continually falling ill. He collapsed more than once while gripping his chest, but the prison administration kept telling him that he suffered from acid reflux. They kept feeding him pills to treat his stomach acid, but his situation worsened with time. It hardly helped that he was severely beaten whenever he stood up for himself or for one of us.

When we learned that we were about to be released as part of a prisoner exchange between the resistance in Gaza and Israel, we were elated. We hugged each other but tried to contain our joy, as we were also deeply saddened for our comrades that we were leaving behind. Majdi had spent more time in prison than I had, nearly 20 years.

When we left prison, we went to Mecca together to perform the Hajj pilgrimage. I wanted to get married and start a family, and he wanted to expand his. But, months later, Majdi realized that his ailment was more serious than previously thought. He was diagnosed with heart disease, a condition that he had endured unknowingly for years in prison. Medical neglect of Palestinian prisoners is all too common in Israeli prisons. By the time doctors in Jordan informed Majdi that he would not survive surgery, and that he should spend the remaining days with his family, he had another child, Mu'tasim, and his wife was pregnant with a third. He had resolved to call him Mohammad.

During that time, a mutual friend suggested that I ask Majdi for his daughter's hand in marriage. I chuckled. I told him Ghadeer was still a teenager. "A teenager in 2002," he said. "Ten years have passed since then, Mohammad."

For us prisoners, time stands still.

It took me a while to imagine that the young teenage girl was all grown up and could possibly be the mother of my children. Later, I sent my mother and sister to ask Majdi and his wife for Ghadeer's hand. Majdi called me the same day. "I could not ask for someone better than you to marry my daughter," he said. When I went to their home in the northern town of Beit Lahia, Ghadeer had broken her leg just two days earlier. She was limping, with a large cast on her leg. I told myself: "I better avoid looking at the cast so as not to make her nervous and just keep looking at her face." She was beautiful and had a kind face. She told me, months after we were married, that, when she first saw my face, she was afraid of me. Maybe it was because of my bushy beard or rough demeanor. But, then, she said, when she saw me conversing with her dad softly, as if I were his younger brother, she immediately decided to accept my proposal.

On the day we agreed to the marriage terms, Majdi hugged me and cried. Then, I cried. I asked him: "What is it about us, Majdi? We cry when we are sad and we cry when we are happy; we cry when we are in prison and when we are free." Then, we all laughed. Soon after my marriage to Ghadeer, Majdi died. I watched him in his last moments hugging his son and Ghadeer. I kissed his forehead and told him not to worry, that his family was now mine and that I would do my best to carry on with his proud legacy for as long as I live.

Now that Majdi is gone, I love Ghadeer ten times more. I feel a great sense of responsibility towards his family, which is now my family. His son, Mohammad, is now like my own son. I called one of my two boys Majdi, after my best friend. I draw strength from Majdi's memory. He helped me cope with the harshness of prison life and his legacy helps me cope with life outside.

—Narrated by Mohammad al-Deirawi

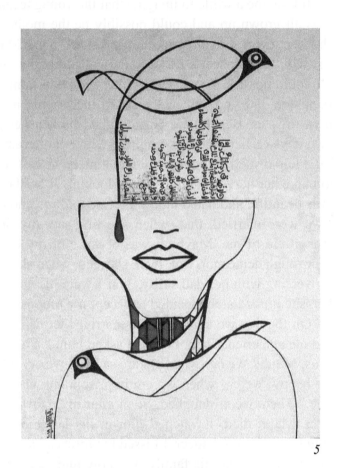

5

And don't always trust your memories
Don't become incandescent in order to light up your mother,
That's her task
Don't hanker for your grandfather's black cloak
Or your grandmother's bribes
Take off like a colt into the world and...
Be who you are wherever you are
Shoulder the burden of your heart
And then come back if your country is really enough to be
*   a country*

—Dareen Tatour

MY BROKEN LEG;
MY SOARING SPIRIT

Dareen Tatour

DAREEN Tatour was born on April 16, 1982 in the Galilee village of Reineh,[22] near the city of Nazareth. She is a member of the Palestinian community that remained in historic Palestine after the ethnic cleansing of most Palestinians by Zionist militias and the establishment of Israel in 1948. Today, this Palestinian community numbers about a fifth of the population of Israel.

Dareen has a degree in computer engineering and has also studied film-making and media.

Dareen is a poet—and a courageous one—a fact that did not sit well with Israeli authorities. She was arrested from her home before dawn on October 11, 2015, by a large number of Israeli army troops and border police. Her interrogation lasted for 21 days, before the Israeli prosecution submitted to the court, on November 2, a list of accusations in which Dareen was charged with inciting violence. The claim was entirely based on a poem she had written and published on social media networks. In the poem, Dareen urged her people to resist the Israeli occupation.

---

22 Reineh is a Palestinian Arab village located north of Nazareth, in the Galilee region.

Dareen spent 97 days in prison before she was placed under house arrest in Tel Aviv, away from her family, for two years and eight months. As soon as that period ended, the Nazareth district court continued to pursue the case against Dareen, sentencing her to an additional five months in prison.

The Palestinian poet was finally released on September 20, 2018, on condition that she would no longer write political poetry. If she was to do so, stipulated the Israeli court, Dareen would face six more months in prison and three more years of house arrest. The case against Dareen has garnered international attention, resulting in her poem being translated and published in over 20 languages.

RESIST, MY PEOPLE, RESIST THEM.

In Jerusalem, I dressed my wounds and
             breathed my sorrows
And carried the soul in my palm
Of an Arab Palestine.
I will not succumb to the "peaceful solution,"
Never lower my flags
Until I evict them from my land.
I cast them aside for a coming time.
Resist, my people, resist them.
Resist the settler's robbery
And follow the caravan of martyrs.
Shred the disgraceful constitution
Which imposed degradation and humiliation
And deterred us from restoring justice.
They burned blameless children;

As for Hadeel,[23] they sniped her in public,
Killed her in broad daylight.
Resist, my people, resist them.
Resist the colonialist's onslaught.
Pay no mind to his agents among us
Who chain us with the peaceful illusion.
Do not fear doubtful tongues;
The truth in your heart is stronger,
As long as you resist in a land
That has lived through raids and victory.
So Ali called from his grave:
Resist, my rebellious people.
Write me as prose on the agarwood;
My remains have you as a response.
Resist, my people, resist them.
Resist, my people, resist them.[24]

———————

IT WAS ON TUESDAY, OCTOBER 22, 2015 AT 6 P.M. that I fell and broke my leg. I was trying to climb down from my bunk bed in my prison cell. All I wanted was to get something from my little closet in the corner. The task, however, was not an easy one.

For days, I repeatedly asked the prison administration to help me. The narrow, metal ladder I needed to climb up to my bed, and down, was blocked by another bed. Getting up or down from my bed was a physical feat, requiring focus

---

23 Hadeel al-Hashlamon was an 18-year-old Palestinian student. She was shot dead by Israeli forces at a checkpoint in Al-Khalil (Hebron) on September 22, 2015. "Young Palestinian Woman Shot by Israeli Forces Dies," *Al Jazeera,* September 22, 2015, <https://www.aljazeera.com/news/2015/09/israeli-forces-shoot-palestinian-woman-west-bank-150922070049785.html>.

24 Translated from Arabic by Tariq al-Haydar.

and time. I suggested to the prison guards to move the ladder from its current position and to fasten it to the opposite side of my bunk bed, a quick way to fix the problem. But the prison administration rejected my demand and kept saying: "Write down your complaint and we will resolve the issue when the time is right."

But that time never came. So, I tried to conjure up an alternative way to resolve the problem. I positioned a small, plastic table at one side of the bunk bed to serve as a stepping stool. For a while, the idea worked. I would stand on the table, and from there climb up to my mattress, as if I were climbing a tree. But on that terrible Tuesday, I fell on my way down. The table was too flimsy and unstable. At first, it wobbled a little and then it suddenly dropped to its side. Unable to hold on to anything, I dived down as well. My whole body slammed to the floor. I was hurting everywhere, but my right ankle was in tremendous pain. I immediately knew that it was broken as I could not move it at all. My cellmates gathered around me in distress. They carried me to the closest bed. I was in agony. I felt as if my right foot was entirely detached from the rest of my body. An initial discoloration around my ankle quickly turned dark blue. My toes, too, turned blue and my whole foot began to swell, eventually looking more like a partially deflated balloon.

My cell mates began yelling to the prison guards for help. A female guard came, and I explained to her in Hebrew that my foot was clearly broken and that I needed to be taken to the hospital. She left, returning a short while later to tell me through the little opening in the door that she had informed the prison administration and that they would look into it.

Nearly two hours later, four people entered: two officers, a medic and another prison guard. One of the two officers asked me what had happened. I told him that I fell but he was not convinced. "Are you sure you were not beaten up by the other prisoners in the room?" I wanted to scream at him, to tell him that we were all sisters and we did not abuse one another, but I was in too much pain to even breathe normally, let alone scream at this repulsive man. "I told you, I fell," I repeated.

Facing the medic, the other officer asked, "How do you assess her case?"

"Nothing serious; we should be able to take care of this at the prison's clinic," the medic said, as he dispassionately examined my foot.

I said, firmly: "My leg is broken. I know that. It requires an actual hospital and an x-ray."

The medic drew closer once more and said: "Wiggle your toes."

"I cannot even touch my toes because of the extreme pain; how can I possibly wiggle them?" I replied.

They all left. Another hour later, the medic came back with a small bag of ice. He said: "Place this on your ankle." He also gave me a pill to manage the pain.

The following day, nearly seven hours later, my pain was excruciating. The discoloring of the foot spread further and the swelling worsened, going up most of my leg, up to my knee. After much crying and, thanks to the persistence of my cellmates, the prison administration relented, allowing me to see a doctor at the clinic.

At the clinic, the doctor examined my foot and spoke to an officer and two guards in a language I am not familiar with. It was probably Russian. I was later told that I would be transferred to a nearby hospital because my foot was in a terrible condition. They also gave me two crutches.

I walked slowly, using the crutches, while surrounded by six soldiers from the army unit responsible for transporting prisoners. I struggled to climb up the stairs of the prison

Illustration by Dareen Tatour | 6

vehicle, known as bosta.[25] As I finally managed to take my seat, located inside a small cage built within the bosta truck, a soldier took my crutches away. A female solider quickly handcuffed me and then she bent down to place shackles on my feet, but I protested: "How can you possibly shackle a broken foot?"

---

25   The "bosta" is the Israeli prison transfer vehicle in which Palestinian prisoners are cuffed all the way to and back from court or clinic while sitting on metal chairs. Some of the prisoners have described the vehicle with blacked-out windows as a "grave." Others have said that it is in fact "a mobile cell with a metal chair that can barely accommodate one person in a sitting position." "The Bosta, a Journey of Endless Pain," The Palestinian Information Center, accessed August 3, 2019, <https://english.palinfo.com/news/2016/12/18/The-Bosta-a-journey-of-endless-pain>.

Her facial expression did not change. She consulted with another soldier, who instructed her to find another way to chain my feet. She returned and placed the shackles on my left foot, then tied them to the metal chair which was attached to the floor inside my cage. Then, she locked the cage and stood guard with the other soldiers.

As the prison vehicle began moving, I thought to myself: one foot broken, another tied to a metal chair; my hands cuffed as I sit inside a cage that feels like a mobile grave, and all that for writing a poem condemning the occupation. Every bump in the road multiplied my pain. No words can truly express how I felt at that moment.

Half an hour later, the vehicle stopped, the door to my cage was opened, and a female soldier brought me a wheelchair, before ordering me to step out of the truck without removing my handcuffs. I had had enough. I told her that I would not move an inch unless they freed my hands. She did. I then stepped out of the truck and down the stairs with the help of my crutches, slowly positioning myself in the wheelchair. As soon as I did, a soldier handcuffed me again, then shackled my left foot to the wheelchair before wheeling me into the emergency ward at Bnei Zion Hospital in Haifa.

I was wheeled into the hospital, accompanied by five soldiers, two walking in front of me, two behind me and one pushing my chair. The x-ray revealed that my foot was, indeed, fractured. Most of my leg was then placed in a cast, before I was taken back to the bosta truck in accordance with the same military protocol: the soldiers, the guns, the handcuffs and the shackles.

Inside the truck, I was placed in my metal cage once again. A female solider cuffed my hands, then knelt down, trying to shackle the cast on my broken foot to the other foot in frustration. The shackles were just too small for a large cast. She tried, again and again. Finally, she gave up, settling for shackling my left foot to the metal chair and locking the door of my cage.

As soon as I returned to my prison cell and lay down on my bed, I took a piece of paper and a pencil, and I penned down another poem because, even if they manage to always cage my body, they will never succeed in containing my soul.

THE PRISONER'S RIDE

Heart entangled on a journey
that seizes all color from life's portrait.

A dark cell, more like a cemetery,
this is the incontrovertible truth.

In a flash I saw my fate on the road,
in a vehicle that's more of a coffin

and I rode it in it and my soul wondered
does it carry the living or deliver them to their
        deaths?

Obscure and chilling, airless
in summer and in winter, outside of time

Named a refrigerator for the living,
In its frigidity my skin scorches.

No light no color nothing to perceive
Utter gloom in its vault.

And how tight the shackles on the ankles
and the chains around the wrists!

Through piercings the glass is visible,
I glimpse the iron bars of this cage.

As for air, it is nonexistent
not even a morsel to grant lungs their breath

And the cursing, ever-present
soldiers compelled to project it at us

Here she is, prisoner embraced by isolation,
without food or water, besieged by darkness

The means of torture by the enemy are multiple
but my spirit is unintimidated by their presence.

No matter how they shackle emotions,
        no matter the despair,
The spirit will not bow down,
        its perseverance will not perish.

No matter how veiled their deception,
my sighs are unrelenting.

For moons to rise in our skies
we have to live through this darkness.[26]

—Dareen Tatour

---

26 Translated from Arabic by Lena Khalaf Tuffaha.

7

I come from there and I have memories
Born as mortals are, I have a mother
And a house with many windows,
I have brothers, friends,
And a prison cell with a cold window.
I learnt all the words worthy of the court of blood
So that I could break the rule.
I learnt all the words and broke them up
To make a single word: Homeland.....

—Mahmoud Darwish

FOR MY LITTLE BROTHER

JALAL Lutfi Saqr was born on January 20, 1963 in the Nuseirat Refugee Camp in Gaza.[27] He is the second of six brothers and sisters. His family originally came from Hamameh, a village in southern Palestine that was depopulated and destroyed by Zionist militias in 1948. The survivors of the village were scattered to many places, most of them living in permanent exile in Gaza's refugee camps.

Saqr married Sumiya Nabhan in 1987 and together they have three daughters, Kansa,'Ala' and Afnan. He was arrested five times, first during the popular uprising, the Intifada, in December 1987, where he was held for 18 days at the notorious Ansar Prison in Gaza. He was detained again in March 1988, when he was kept, along with all of his brothers, in administrative detention for three months. In July 1988, he was imprisoned for 18 more days, and in July 1990, his detention was extended for three months, this time in Ansar III Prison[28] in the Naqab Desert.

---

27   According to UNRWA, "the Nuseirat refugee camp is currently home to more than 80,194 refugees. Like Bureij and Maghazi refugee camps, Nuseirat camp is located in the middle of the Gaza Strip." UNRWA, accessed July 31, 2019, <https://www.unrwa.org/where-we-work/gaza-strip/nuseirat-camp>.

28   See Appendix.

On April 8, 1992, Saqr was arrested inside Israel, along with Tariq Dukhan. He was wounded in both feet in a confrontation with Israeli soldiers. He was tried in a military court and later sentenced to 400 years in prison for his role in establishing Al-Qassam Brigades, the military wing of the Hamas movement.

NAEL WAS ONLY 18 WHEN I WAS ARRESTED. He was the youngest in the family. He was spoiled and quite a beautiful boy, always well dressed and full of life. He loved school ever since he was in the first grade. After high school, he joined Birzeit University, where he studied Anthropology. As soon as he graduated, he worked at the Ministry of Social Affairs, focusing mostly on helping the families of martyrs to cope with life after their tragedy and loss. People loved him and he internalized everyone's pain as if it were his own.

He was allowed to visit me in prison only once, in 2000, nearly ten years after my arrest. I was impressed with the man he grew up to be, articulate, intelligent and so very mature. He assured me just before he left: "Brother, don't worry about your girls. We will care for them with our eyes and will raise them to be the finest of people."

I never saw him again after that.

At the start of the second uprising, Al-Aqsa Intifada, he got married and God granted him a daughter, Lina, and a son, Majd. He was so happy and grateful for the life God had chosen for him. But things quickly changed.

On February 17, 2002, I was on my way to a seminar to study computer programming, a course that was taught by a Jordanian prisoner who was proficient in the subject. Before I reached the room where the seminar was held, I was stopped by another prisoner, Fouad Abu Amrin, who comes from the same refugee camp as I.

"Is Nael Saqr related to you?" he asked.

"He is my brother, but why do you ask?" I replied.

Fouad was caught by surprise by my answer. He just froze and did not elaborate, not even with one word.

"What's the matter?" I repeated.

But Fouad just stared at the ground and continued to say nothing.

Around that time, we had smuggled a small cell phone into the prison, which all 360 of us took turns in using when we made secret calls to our families. By chance, it was Fouad's turn to use the device. While talking to his family earlier, they informed him that a large procession had circled the camp on that day, carrying the body of a young man named Nael Saqr. I refused to believe that it was my brother. Nuseirat is far away from the Israeli border where most of the clashes usually happen, I insisted. It could not be my brother. It must have been someone else with the same name.

Only the day before, it had been my turn to use the cell phone. I had phoned my family and checked on everyone by name. "All is well," they assured me. Nael was fine just yesterday. So, I gave my family's number to Fouad and I urged him to call my family as soon as there was a signal. Hours later, he came looking for me with a look on his face that I will never forget. "Your brother has been martyred," he said. I immediately knelt down, then placed my forehead to the ground, crying but also thanking God for honoring my brother with martyrdom. I told my comrades in prison: "Don't console me but congratulate me; my brother died proud, with his head held high."

When I managed to contact my family, I discovered that Nael's body was still at the mosque, being readied for the final prayer before burial in the Martyrs' Graveyard. Using the smuggled cell phone, I spoke to the mourners at the mosque and urged them to remain steadfast. "Ours is a long and painful march for freedom," I told them. "Some of us are in prison; others are under the ground, but we will never cease our fight for our people. We must remain committed to the legacy of our forefathers and our martyrs. We are all brothers, in blood, in the struggle and in faith, so let's remain united as one people, as brothers and sisters, and carry on despite the heavy losses and tremendous sacrifices."

My brother died fighting, on his feet, not on his knees. He was attempting, with a group of youth, to block the advancement of Israeli tanks east of Bureij,[29] another refugee camp that is adjacent to ours. They tried to slow down the movement of the Israeli army so that people could evacuate their neighborhoods for safer areas. But he was shot in the head, shattering part of his skull and causing internal bleeding in the brain. He died soon afterwards from his wounds at the Shifa Hospital in Gaza.

When Nael died, I vowed that if I was ever to regain my freedom, I would dedicate my life to raising his two children, the way he had helped me raise my own.

My beautiful girls. They were my only reason for hope in my long years in prison. When I was arrested in 1992, my eldest daughter, Khansa,' was only three and a half, Ala' was a year and a half and Afnan was only five months old. I was barely getting comfortable with the role of being a father when all of this was interrupted. Throughout much of my 20 years in prison, I was denied visitation. In the last ten years of my stay, my family was only allowed to see me five times, and if my mom made it to the prison, my wife and kids were denied from joining her. If my wife and

---

29   "Bureij refugee camp is a comparatively small refugee camp located in the middle of the Gaza Strip." UNRWA, accessed August 1, 2019, <https://www. unrwa.org/where-we-work/gaza-strip/bureij-camp>.

kids made it, my mom was prevented from seeing me. My happiness in seeing them was never complete.

Khansa' married in 2008, and Ala' a year later. It was tormenting, picturing my girls in their white wedding dresses while I was not there to hold their hands, greet the guests and feel proud of what they had become. I longed to hold them in my arms. It pained me that I missed out on everything: their first day at school, their graduation, even their weddings. I wondered if they were happy or if they missed me too much, if they were scared or felt vulnerable without me by their side, especially now that their uncle Nael was dead.

When it was Afnan's turn to get married in 2010, there were rumors that a prisoner exchange between the resistance and Israel was about to take place. Her fiancé spoke to me in prison. He said that they had talked about it and they would be happy to postpone the wedding as long as it would take, until I was out of prison so that I could attend the ceremony. I told him to go ahead and not to wait for me.

A few days later, I saw Afnan on the Al-Aqsa TV channel. She said: "I wish my Daddy could be with me on my wedding day." Tears fell from my eyes as I watched her, so beautiful, so articulate and proud. The Gaza Prime Minister at the time, Ismail Haniyeh, heard her on TV and volunteered to stand in my place at the wedding. I appreciated that gesture very much.

My comrades in prison realized how depressed I was that I could not be with my youngest daughter on her wedding day. So they arranged for a video call to my family. The line did not connect despite numerous attempts, but when I was about to give up, just for a split second, a video appeared and then froze at an image of Afnan in her white wedding dress. I could not believe that my baby was married. I was happy, but heartbroken. I kept reminding myself: "This is the cost of defending one's homeland; freedom is precious and fighting for freedom can be most painful. But, inshallah, I will see her and all of my children soon and make up for all the lost time."

A year later, I was released in a prisoner exchange. I felt that it was a new opportunity for me to reclaim my role, not just as a father but as a grandfather as well, now that I had 11 grandchildren. I want to be there for all of them, every step of the way. I want to attend every graduation and every wedding and every celebration. I am also back in my refugee camp, taking my part in the struggle of my people as they endure for the sake of their freedom and liberation.

The love for my family and the solidarity of my community made up for much of the suffering I endured in prison. But one cannot be truly free when thousands of our people are still in prison, when Gaza is under siege, when Palestine is occupied.

As soon as I left prison, I went to Nael's grave. It is adorned with the colors of the Palestinian flag and verses from the Holy Quran. I told my little brother how much I loved and appreciated him, and that, one day, we would meet again in paradise.

8

AVENGING SABRA AND SHATILA

Kifah Sobhi 'Afifi

KIFAH Sobhi 'Afifi was born in the Shatila refugee camp in south Lebanon on October 27, 1970. Her family, refugees from the town of Yajour, near Haifa,[30] was ethnically cleansed along with hundreds of thousands of Palestinians during Al-Nakba—the destruction of the historical Palestinian homeland by Zionist militias in 1947-48.

Kifah's family consisted of six sisters and five brothers. Her father, a fighter with the Popular Front for the Liberation of Palestine (PFLP), was wounded when their home was bombed during an Israeli assault on the area, but he remained active in the camps, and especially in Shatila. Her mother was one of the leading female activists in the camp. She kept busy standing guard whenever PFLP fighters met in the camp. She would also bring food and weapons to fighters in the besieged areas. During the war, she played a vital role in the camps, supporting the fighters on the front

---

30 The Palestinian town of Yajur was located 5.9 miles (9.5 kilometers) southeast of the city of Haifa. Its Palestinian inhabitants were ethnically cleansed on April 25, 1948. The town was subsequently destroyed. Palestine Remembered, accessed August 1, 2019, <https://www.palestineremembered.com/Haifa/Yajur/index.html>.

lines. Three of her brothers, Yousef, Khaled and Othman were killed during Lebanon's "war of the camps."[31]

Kifah is now married to Mohammed Ramadan, with whom she has four children. She lives with her family in the Cola area in Beirut.

In October 1988, Kifah participated in a resistance operation against the Israeli occupation army near the Fatima Gate, located between Israel and Lebanon. The objective was to capture an Israeli soldier and exchange him for Palestinian prisoners. However, she was wounded in the ensuing clashes. She was captured, detained and tortured by the Israeli army. She spent seven years in the Khiam prison[32] and was released at the beginning of 1995, along with three other female prisoners, as part of a prisoners' exchange.

———————

I WAS BORN WITHOUT A HOMELAND. As a child, I do not recall ever purchasing a toy. My family was too poor to provide such seemingly luxurious items. Our household never experienced real stability. My father was consumed with the thought of someday going back to his hometown, Yajour, in Palestine. All of us were. Violence engulfed our very existence. We woke up to the smell of gunpowder and fell asleep to the sound of bombs. Even as a very young child, I witnessed death with my own eyes far too many times. I

---

31   "Between 1985 and 1989, Lebanon was the scene of what became known as the Camps War, when pro-Syrian militiamen from Amal, a Lebanese Shia movement, and anti-(late Palestinian leader Yasser) Arafat factions laid siege to Palestinian refugee camps in Beirut and the south. Palestinian refugees suffered grim atrocities, and according to journalist Robert Fisk, the Camps War "was worse than the Sabra and Shatila massacre." "Lebanon's Palestinian Refugees," *Al Jazeera*, June 4, 2019, <https://www.aljazeera.com/focus/2009/05/2009527115531294628.html>.

32   See Appendix.

have escaped death repeatedly. Since I was a teenager, I was determined to join the armed resistance. I eventually did.

I memorized the map of Palestine as soon as I learned the alphabet. I knew the geography of Palestine from memory, and I knew precisely where Yajour was located on the map of Palestine. We long for Palestine, because our homeland is molded into our identity as a people. Our life in the camp was that of poverty and neglect and, with time, it got much worse.

When the Massacre of Sabra and Shatila[33] took place in September 1982, I was only 12 years old. We were all at home when, suddenly, military flares lit up the sky, followed by continuous bombing. We began running towards my sister's home. But the bombing worsened and was approaching her neighborhood as well, so we ran together to the shelter. I remember holding a blue rug between my arms. I refused to let go of it because I did not want to sit on the dirty floor.

Once we reached the shelter, a delegation of old men from the camp offered to appeal to the Israeli army, to implore them to cease the bombing and to explain that we have no men amongst us. As they left, my brother, Othman, followed them. A short while later, he came running back, screaming: "They killed the old men! They killed all of them!"

We panicked. If the old men were massacred, no one was safe. Not knowing where else to go, we rushed to the Rihab mosque in the camp. All of us were screaming and

---

33 With direct help from the Israeli army, on September 16, 1982, the Christian Phalange militia stormed the Sabra and Shatila refugee camps in Beirut, killing between 3,000-3,500 Palestinian refugees. "The Sabra & Shatila Massacre," Global Research, accessed August 3, 2019, <https://imeu.org/article/the-sabra-shatila-massacrehttps://www.globalresearch.ca/israeli-crimes-against-humanity-remembering-the-sabra-and-shatila-massacre/5545969>.

wailing: "Oh Allah, oh Merciful, please help us! What have we done to deserve this?"

The Israeli soldiers began yelling at us over loudspeakers. We felt that the sound was drawing near and we had no idea what to do or where to escape. A young man by the name of Mansour rushed our way and instructed us to run in the opposite direction, since the Israelis and the militias were closing in. So we ran, trying to stay as close to the walls of the camp as possible. That is when I saw the piles of dead bodies all around. Children, women and men, mutilated or groaning in pain as they were dying. Bullets were flying everywhere. People were falling all around me. I saw a father using his body to protect his children, but they were all shot and killed, anyway.

Finally, we managed to take shelter in a little sewing shop where refugee women from the camp worked to make some extra income. We knew that our hideout was not safe and that we would eventually be found and killed, so we decided to run again and seek shelter in the Gaza Hospital. My aunt and her family came with us as well. She had a baby daughter who was crying from hunger. My aunt and her husband ventured out to find some milk, but they were both killed by the Israeli army. We have never located their bodies as they were buried in one mass grave with many other people.

Eventually, we left the hospital, running from one building to the next. However, we were caught by the Israeli army and taken to the stadium,[34] where people were lined up and shot, one group after the other. Many were massacred in front of me, as my family and I were waiting our turn to be killed. However, some people were spared, and we

_____

34   "Survivors recount Sabra-Shatila Massacre," *Al Jazeera,* September 16, 2012, <https://www.aljazeera.com/indepth/features/2012/09/20129151631522213255.html>.

were ordered by the army to leave in one specific direction, otherwise, they said, they would kill us like the rest. Exhausted and hungry, we finally settled near the electric company, to be subjected to daily searches as the Israelis and their collaborators were looking for men. Any man who was found among the refugees was immediately executed.

The events of these few days are etched in my memory, and the passage of time will never change or alter them in any way. I became obsessed with avenging my loved ones, my innocent friends and neighbors. My parents raised us to be as rooted in our identity and love for our homeland as the olive tree. My family suffered so much for merely being Palestinian and for seeking to return to their homeland.

Three years later, in 1985, the war on the camps resumed, once the Israeli occupation was complete. Israel's collaborators in Lebanon wanted to finish the job. They were out to target Palestinians and anyone who dared to resist the occupation. My brother, Yousef, was the first to be killed in 1985. He was bringing weapons to Shatila when he was captured, tortured and then cut into pieces. His body was not recognizable by our family. Yousef was buried in a mass grave with 90 other bodies. His death was followed by Khaled's in 1987, and then that of Othman in 1988. My brother, Mohammed, was also arrested in 1986. He endured brutal physical and psychological torture.

It was during those years that I resolved to join the resistance. In the mid-1980s, when I was a teenager, I enlisted as a fighter with the Fatah movement. I swore to follow the legacy of Dalal Mughrabi,[35] who has been my hero ever since I was a child. I underwent various training programs before

---

35 Dalal Mughrabi was a Palestinian female freedom fighter belonging to the Palestine Liberation Organization (PLO). Al-Mughrabi was killed on March 11, 1978, during a military operation that she led inside Israel. "Palestinian Women's Center to Keep Name Despite Pressure from UN," Norway, Ma'an, May 30, 2017, <https://www.maannews.com/Content.aspx?id=777396>.

I began taking part in resistance operations targeting Israeli occupation soldiers. I was not afraid of death. My only wish was that, if I was to be a martyr, it would be while I was defending the precious soil of my homeland, Palestine, the land of my parents and my ancestors.

I was 17 years old when I was arrested on October 24, 1988 in the region of Kafr Kala in south Lebanon. I was trying to cross the Lebanon-Palestine border with six other fighters in order to reach the northern regions of Palestine. Our objective was to kidnap Israeli soldiers and exchange them for Palestinian prisoners. It is there that I was captured and then sent to interrogation.

After hours of being questioned and tortured by the Lahad Army,[36] I was thrown into a jeep. I heard the soldiers saying that they would take me to one of the settlements in northern Palestine to be interrogated. I was ecstatic at the thought of actually entering Palestine, even under these conditions. From the time I was a child, so many people told me: "When you enter Palestine, all you can smell is the perfume of roses," and they were right! As soon as we approached the border, I was overwhelmed with the beautiful scent of roses. I cried out: "I am in Palestine!" I was overcome with joy and began singing. The soldiers cursed me and said that I was in Israel, not Palestine. They stopped the jeep, blindfolded me and taped my mouth shut. Many of the Israeli soldiers there posed with me, taking photos. Their interrogation and torture was horrific, but I am proud to say that, although I endured so much cruelty from them, I did not confess to anything or answer any of their questions.

---

36 The South Lebanon Army (SLA), led by General Antoine Lahad, was a Lebanese militia that was armed, trained and financed by Israel. The SLA, along with Israeli troops, controlled what they called the "security zone" in south Lebanon. "The Cost of Collaboration," *Al Jazeera,* May 26, 2010, <https://www. aljazeera.com/focus/2010/05/201051992011673189.html>.

After one short day in my beloved homeland, I was thrown back into the jeep and was brought across the border again to south Lebanon, where I would spend the next seven years in Khiam Prison, known as the "Prison of Death." Even though I was 17 years old, I was of very small stature, so the Israelis thought I was not older than 13. I had never heard of this prison prior to my arrest. I was unaware that I would spend the next seven years in a prison unrecognized internationally, where neither the Red Cross nor families of detainees were allowed visitation. Once you were confined in this place, you effectively went missing; you were completely isolated from the rest of the world and no one knew anything about you. The lack of any form of international control made it easy for Israel's collaborators, the Lahad Army—which administered Khiam Prison—to use all forms of psychological and physical torture against the detainees. Within the cells of the prison, anything and everything was allowed.

During the first part of my imprisonment and interrogation, my jailers used all kinds of psychological torture. When I refused to give them information, they threatened to rape me. They said they would "teach me what a man does to a woman." They brought in a huge man with blue eyes to rape me. When he made two attempts, I said: "If you want to rape me, go ahead; you raped my land and my people, so go ahead and rape me." After that, they left me alone. But they did not stop there. They put me into an animal cage, poured gasoline all over the cage and threatened to burn me alive. They also brought in dogs to attack the cage.

My torturers' favorite techniques included burning me with cigarettes and electrocuting my body. To do that, they would wire my chest, and then turn on a high electric voltage. Whenever they did that, I felt that my soul was about to depart my body. But I did my utmost to hide my pain from them. I did not want to give them the satisfaction that they were seeking. Outraged by my defiance, they tied me to another chair, one that is made entirely of metal. Then they poured cold water on my body before electrocuting me again. This time the pain was unbearable. My body could no longer fight back. I fell unconscious, only to be awakened by a group of men beating me. I spent many days under this excruciating routine.

Although I was the youngest prisoner and the only Palestinian, I never hesitated to help other prisoners, and this got me into a lot of trouble. It is in my nature to hate injustice; I could not keep silent about the injustice exacted against us.

It pains me to think of the physical and psychological torture and humiliation my sisters and I endured while we were in prison. Because I had a particularly defiant nature, my jailers always attempted to break my spirit. I was intentionally tortured on all levels, particularly during my menstrual cycle. My jailers made sure that everyone knew that I was having my period: the police, the investigators, those in charge of the prison. The Israelis would torture me most during this time. They refused to provide me with sanitary pads, so I would cut blankets into small pieces to use. Other prisoners would give me their clothes to cut up to use, as well.

The relationship among the sisters in prison was exceptional. We were truly a family. I am so proud of my prison mates. We had an inexplicable power to face life in prison. We made trivial things, handwork and paintings, which were always confiscated by our jailers. Those who knew languages taught the rest of us. The sisters who could read and write taught those who were illiterate. We celebrated birthdays, and all sorts of holidays together, using our humble means.

I did not just see prison as a place of pain, but as an arena for sumoud, or steadfastness. It was a mere station on the path of resistance against Israel and its collaborators. My Israeli torturers could not silence me, even when I was strapped to a chair, blood pouring out of my mouth while repeatedly being jolted with electricity. I challenged them even then. I spoke out for the rights of my sisters in prison.

Prison never killed the rebellion in my heart. On the contrary, it cemented my belief in my cause and my love for my homeland. After leaving Khiam Prison, I married the man of my dreams, a freed prisoner, Mohammed Ramadan. He is Lebanese, but his heart and mind are always in Palestine. Mohammed spent nine years in Khiam after taking part in a resistance operation against Israeli soldiers. Mohammed and I were married on July 27, 1996. We now have three daughters and one son.

My body is now frail and exhausted. Living in a refugee camp, experiencing war, torture and prison leaves you with many scars that only worsen with time, but my love for Palestine remains as strong as ever. I think of all the prisoners who are suffering, as I did. I relive my pain when I hear their stories.

For years, I have dedicated my life to raising awareness about the plight of Palestinian prisoners. I take part in every event, vigil or protest in solidarity with our heroic prisoners in Israeli jails. I often travel outside Lebanon to tell the world about the suffering and steadfastness of those who are held and tortured by Israel.

I am still exiled—a refugee. Israel will not allow me to simply visit my homeland. But I am full of hope and determination that I, and all the refugees, will someday go back to Palestine. I am sure of this fact more than anything else in this world. We will continue to fight for our right of return, until we make it a reality.

—Kifah Sobhi 'Afifi

9

ME AND ISLAM

Mohammad Mohammad Abu Hasira

MOHAMMAD Mohammad Abu Hasira was born on May 6, 1971 in the city of Gaza, where his family lived for many generations. He is the third of nine siblings, five sisters and four brothers.

Abu Hasira married Nuha Abu Kamal in December 1991. They had a daughter, Islam. When Abu Hasira was arrested from his home in Gaza on October 29, 1993, Islam was only six months old. He was accused of establishing militant cells and resisting the Israeli army in the Gaza Strip. He was sentenced to 337 years in prison.

Abu Hasira spent 20 years in Israeli prisons. Throughout these years, the thought of Islam sustained him. From the interrogation room in Saraya Prison,[37] to the pre-trial years in Askalan, to his seemingly endless isolation in Nafha, his daughter, Islam, was always on his mind.

He was released on October 18, 2011.

———————

ISLAM WAS ONLY SIX MONTHS OLD when I was arrested in October 1993. I spent the first months of my imprisonment

---

37 See Appendix.

in the Saraya Prison in central Gaza. I was not able to see my daughter for months. She grew during that time from being a baby to being a little girl. When she came to visit me for the first time, along with my wife and mother, I did not recognize her. She was running around happily without a care in the world. "Whose child is this?" I asked them. My wife and Mom began crying. They told me that she was my daughter, Islam. I cursed the occupation for keeping my family from me for a long time.

For the first three years, I was moved from one prison to another. This took place during my interrogation and court hearings. During that time, I rarely saw Islam or my wife and mother. My love for Islam deepened with time, especially as my wife, who was pregnant when I was arrested, lost the baby. The Israeli army kept raiding our house and arresting members of my family. The constant trauma and fear made my wife collapse. Subsequent severe bleeding at a Gaza hospital made her lose our second child.

For 20 years, I dreamed of Islam. Her beautiful face, her innocence and her love for life was my main motivator. She visited me in my dreams, and the thought of her accompanied me throughout my day. The few times that I saw her, I was never allowed to hold her or even touch her little hand. I saw her growing up from behind thick glass walls. Three years after my initial arrest, however, I was finally allowed to be with her, but only for 20 minutes.

When I first held her in my arms, I drew her close to my heart, and I felt that all the longing and loneliness that I had suffered had been quenched. I felt that I was holding my own heart and soul between my hands. My beautiful, pure little Islam, with me after all of these years. All the darkness of my cell, the long years of torture and interrogation had been erased. For a moment, I felt complete. The entire time I spent together with her, I tried to hold back my tears. My wife and Mom could not. I had to play the role of the strong husband and son, but I felt a piercing pain in my chest and guts. When they left, I went back to my cell. I did not want to eat or talk to anyone. I just wanted to savor the echoes of the voices of my family, especially the simple sentences and giggles of my daughter. That night, I went to sleep covering my face with my hands, so that my comrades could not see me crying.

When Islam started first grade, the kids in her class called her "the prisoner's daughter." She was embarrassed, as she was too young to understand that I was not a criminal, and that I had done nothing wrong but defend my people. She went to the principal's office more than once, sobbing because of the name calling. But when the school administration knew who I was and why I was in prison, they gathered all the students and explained to them that "Islam's father is a hero." Islam became the most popular kid at school. When my wife told me the story, I felt happy that, despite my situation, I could still be a source of pride for my daughter.

Prison makes you age fast, and I did. As time passed, my expectations began to change as well. At first, all I wanted was just to hold my daughter close to me, but, with time, I began thinking more about her future, her education and marriage. Islam told her mother that she would not get married until I was freed. I told them not to link Islam's happiness with my freedom, since I did not know if I would ever be free. But I told my wife to choose Islam's husband very carefully. That he must be kind to her, and respectful and caring. Indeed, in 2008, Islam married a good young man. Every attempt of mine to talk to her on her wedding day failed. The comrades in prison tried for hours to find a signal so that I may speak to her over the cell phone that we managed to smuggle into prison. But that did not work.

Instead, I spent the whole day praying for her, that her life would be beautiful, happy and successful.

That smuggled cell phone was my only lifeline. Halfway into my time in prison, I managed, along with other comrades, to obtain a cell phone that was smuggled into our cells. It cost us a large sum of money, but, for me, it was worth it, because it allowed me to check on my family and on Islam. We used the most ingenious ways to hide the phones, as the Israelis used sophisticated technologies to find them, but for the longest time, they failed. At times we hid our phone under a tile on the floor. Carefully, we removed the tile and dug just little bits of dirt at a time so as not to raise suspicion. We also hid it in a book by cutting enough pages in a perfect triangular shape, enough to fit a small cell phone. The Israeli guards would search our books time and time again, without locating the devices. When it was my turn to have the phone, I hid it behind the switch plate. It took me three months to engineer that operation in advance. I took a tiny piece of cement at a time from behind the switch plate, before creating the perfect hiding place. For three years, the Israelis went crazy trying to find our phone, but they could not.

When I made my first call to my wife, she could not believe her ears that it was me. Regrettably, she could not hear me very well. Our house is located in a somewhat isolated area, west of Gaza. The only way my wife and I could talk was for her to climb up to the roof, and, even then, we could barely hear each other. The signal could only be maintained for one minute at a time, and, whenever it cut off, the comrades would have to restore it by blocking the devices that the Israelis used to jam the signal. They used all sorts of creative ways to do that.

Before a call was placed, a prisoner would stand guard, watching the main gate and the movement of the guards. We had been caught red-handed before. Once, in the middle of winter, they suspected that we were making calls; they dragged us all into the prison yard, almost completely naked, and kept us there for 6 hours in the night. It was a harrowing experience. When we were allowed back into our cells, everything in our rooms was confiscated, save a single blanket for each prisoner. If they happened to locate a smuggled item, a single prisoner would take responsibility for it, so that the rest of us could be spared the collective punishment. That prisoner would be kept in isolation for a long time.

The first question I would ask my wife whenever we spoke is "How is Islam?" But I never asked to speak to Islam. I was frightened by the idea of my only daughter getting sick, standing in the cold air on the roof of our house just to talk to me. My wife said many times that "Islam is desperate to talk to you," but I always said "no." "What if she fell as she tried to climb up to the roof? If she doesn't fall, she will be too tired of the effort." I cherished the thought of Islam peacefully laying in her bed, happy and warm and far away from all dangers.

I finally met Islam in 2011 when I was freed. I saw her with her husband at the Rafah crossing, as we were allowed to enter Gaza through Egypt. The six-month-old baby I left behind was a grown woman, married with two children. She named her first born, Mohammad, after me.

I left prison through the will of God and now I am living in the company of my supportive wife, with whom I have four more children: Norhan, six, Maram, five, Hamza, four, and Hazim, three. My beautiful firstborn, Islam, is now 26 years old. She has had more children since then. Aside from Mohammad, she also has Lian, Hamdi and Qusei.

My parents, now in their eighties, are too old and frail. I try to spend as much time in their company as I can, to make up for some of their suffering when I was in prison. There is a new generation that should be rising, ready to take on the responsibility for our fight for freedom. I look at my children and my Islam's children, and I see the future, promising and hopeful.

But nothing in the world equals my beautiful Islam. She is my pride and joy in this life.

—Mohammad Mohammad Abu Hasira

THE GIRL WHO DID NOTHING

DIMA Ismail Rashid al-Wawi was born on November 20, 2003 in the town of Halhul, north of Al-Khalil (Hebron) in the Occupied West Bank. She is the youngest of six sisters and three brothers. Her family earns its income mostly from farming a small piece of land located on the outskirts of the town.

Halhul has been a constant target for Israeli army raids, as its residents have protested against the confiscation of much of their land to support the expansion of the illegal Jewish settlement of Karmei Tzur. Since 2000, the Israeli military has confiscated about 1,500 dunums of land belonging to Halhul, which is subject to routine closures imposed by the Israeli army.

Halhul is almost entirely suffocated. While the illegal settlement blocks the residents' movement north, an Israeli military base and "Jewish-only" by-pass roads isolate the town from all other directions. With military checkpoints and iron gates, the residents of Halhul are trapped and isolated from their natural surroundings.[38]

---

38 "High Level of Violence by Israeli Settlers; Rise in Israeli Fatalities," United Nations Office for the Coordination of Human Affairs, accessed on August 4, 2019, <https://www.ochaopt.org/content/high-level-violence-israeli-settlers-rise-israeli-fatalities>.

Dima has been witness to much of the violence and injustice meted out against her town, although her family tried to protect her and her siblings. On February 9, 2016, Dima was "arrested" by an armed, illegal Jewish settler who claimed that the 12-year-old girl was trying to stab him. After weeks of interrogation by the Israeli army, a military court sentenced her to four and a half months in prison.

Throughout her interrogation, Dima kept telling Israeli officers: "Ma'miltish ishi," "I didn't do anything."

———————

I HAD A TERRIBLE HEADACHE. I did not know what to do. One of my sisters said: "Mom is working in the field; go and see if she will take you to the clinic." I did not know exactly where our land was. We rarely went there; only Mom, Dad and my older siblings did. The younger kids, like me, stayed home, because the Jewish settlers always harassed my family and my parents wanted us to be safe. All I knew is that our land was located near the Jewish settlement. I thought if I reached the settlement first, I could easily find my mom.

Our piece of land is small. It used to be bigger, but the Jewish settlement kept growing in size and kept eating at the land around it, land that belonged not only to Halhul, but to Beit Ummar as well.

When I got close to the settlement, I could not find my mom or any of my family. I was desperate. I started walking hurriedly, at times even running, while looking everywhere. Suddenly an armed man charged at me. He pushed me to the ground and pointed a gun at me. He then ordered me to lie face down, stepped on my back and tied my hands together. After that, he blindfolded me. I was crying really hard, but no one could hear me. Later, a group of Israeli soldiers arrived and threw me into the back of an army vehicle.

I was only 12 years old when this happened. They accused me of trying to stab a settler. It is a complete lie. The settler made that up to justify the way he treated me. They placed me in a very dark room. It was the first time in my life that I slept away from my mom and my family. I was very scared. I thought to myself: "What if they keep me in prison my whole life?" I felt so bad for my mom. She did not know where I was. She was running all over the area calling my name.

They transferred me to HaSharon Prison.[39] There were screams and loud noises coming from everywhere. The Israeli officer who interrogated me told me that I would be imprisoned for a long time. I was so shocked to hear that. I never thought I would endure such an experience. I had heard of this happening to other kids, but I had no idea that it would happen to me, too. I did not know that the occupation was so criminal and so unfair to this extent. But I told myself: "Dima, you have to be strong and face your reality the way it is."

Then, seven large officers entered the room and began interrogating me all at the same time. I was afraid. I kept repeating: "Ma'miltish ishi," "I didn't do anything." But they kept asking, swearing at me and yelling in my face, from morning until the evening hours. Before they left, they tied me to a chair that did not even have legs. I tried so hard to find a comfortable position. It was impossible. I stayed that way until after midnight.

Days passed without my being able to see my family. Only a long time later, my mom was allowed to see me. I was missing my dad, my brothers and my sisters, but just seeing my mother's beautiful face made me happy. She held me close to her the whole time. Her embrace is always so

---

39 See Appendix.

warm. But then, she had to leave. When she did, I felt that my soul and my heart left with her.

I was tried before a military court in the Ofer Prison.[40] I kept telling them that all the accusations were a lie. However, the judge did not listen to me and sentenced me to four and a half months in prison. Back at HaSharon Prison, they placed me with a child around my age. Her name is Malik Salman. We were in the same prison with all the Israeli women criminals. Later, they moved us to the part of the prison where the Palestinian women were held.

I spent a lot of time talking to the prisoners. They were women who were recovering from wounds and others who were young, like me, although I was the youngest in prison at the time. There were mothers separated from their children, and children needing to be with their families. There was a woman named Israa' Ja'abis.[41] Her body was completely burned. I felt so sorry for her, although she was very strong. She looked after me.

One night, I could not sleep. I kept hearing what sounded like the voice of a man being tortured. He was screaming in pain and asking for God's help. I barely slept for a few minutes before I had a terrible nightmare. I woke up screaming, fell off the bed and hurt my neck, which started to bleed. I was too scared to say anything, so I just kept my hand on my neck to stop the blood.

My mattress was very thin, and my pillow was too high. It was so hard to fall asleep, no matter how hard I tried. Everything around me was made of metal and everything was very cold. The food was terrible, and prison guards yelled at us constantly and treated us badly. They would come and order us to stand side by side for a count whenever they

---

40   See Appendix.

41   See chapter, "'No Pain Like Mine,'" p. 155.

pleased. Those who were not available right away would be thrown into solitary confinement.

I served two and a half months of my sentence. The night I was released, an Israeli interrogator summoned me to a room and told me that I would be receiving a life term in prison. I collapsed and began crying, but then they released me the next day. I had no idea what was happening most of the time. In the courts, they spoke Hebrew. They yelled and swore at me all the time. All I knew was that I was in prison for something I did not do.

When I finally knew that I would be released, I tried to recall everything that had happened, to make sense of that terrifying experience. I counted the minutes, even the seconds, separating me from being with my family. At last, soldiers came, handcuffed and shackled me and took me to the bosta. But, instead of dropping me in Halhul, they left me at a military checkpoint in Tulkarm. They thought no one would care to greet me there, but hundreds of people turned out. They came from Halhul, Tulkarm and all over the West Bank. They all hugged me, kissed me, held me on their shoulders and chanted my name and for Palestinian freedom. When I finally got to see my family, I embraced my mom and dad at once. They kissed me all over. I was so happy to be free again, but I could not stop thinking of all the women who were still in prison. They had treated me as though they were all my mothers.

After I was released, on April 26, 2016, I returned to the Halhul Martyrs School. It was wonderful to be back, and I cannot wait to finish my education and become a journalist, carrying the message of the prisoners and their suffering to the world. I want to show the world how the children of Palestine are mistreated every day by the occupation.

Finally, I would like to send a simple message to the free peoples of this world. Please keep Palestine in your heart. Think of the children who are oppressed and who will continue to be oppressed until this unjust occupation ends.

—Dima Ismail al-Wawi

11

DECODING THE WORLD OUTSIDE

Hilal Mohammad Jaradat

HILAL Mohammad Jaradat was born on November 9, 1966 in the town of Yamoun, northwest of Jenin in the West Bank. He is the fifth in a large family of five brothers and four sisters.

His younger brother, Jalal, was only 11 years old when he was deliberately run over by a Jewish settler in the town of Jenin in 1980. He was playing, when the settler drove his car through the crowd of children near the Jenin Road. Jalal was killed instantly. The settler never stood trial for Jalal's murder.

His other young brother, Bilal, was 15 years old when he was drowned at the hands of an Israeli extremist in 1982. Bilal was swimming with friends on a beach in the northern Israeli city of Netanya.[42] The Israeli culprit was never tried for his action.

Hilal and Bilal were very close. When Bilal was killed, Hilal joined the local resistance against the Israeli occupation. He was arrested on August 17, 1985, and, for his

---

42   Netanya is built on the ruins of the Palestinian city of Umm Khalid. Palestine Remembered, accessed July 31, 2019, <https://www.palestineremembered.com/Tulkarm/Umm-Khalid/index.html>.

membership in the military wing of Fatah, he was sentenced by an Israeli military court in Nazareth to one year in prison. He was arrested once more on September 24, 1987, this time accused of taking part in a military operation that resulted in the killing of three armed Jewish settlers.

Hilal was 20 years of age at the time of his arrest.

Hilal's mother, Tamam, was heartbroken after the loss of two of her children, and the sentencing of a third. Two years later, she fell ill and died. Hilal's old, ailing father was the only person allowed to see him in prison. He did so regularly at first but, later, he was too frail to undergo the arduous journey.

When Hilal was finally released from prison, in 2011, he was 46 years of age. A year later, he met Nuha. They are now married and have two children: a girl, Jenin, six, and a boy, Mohammed, four.

Hilal was deported from the West Bank as soon as he was released from the Naqab Prison[43] and is currently living in the Nuseirat Refugee Camp in Gaza.

He spends his time looking after his family, teaching languages and reading.

I WAS SENTENCED TO 303 YEARS IN PRISON, a long time for a person to be on his own doing nothing. When I was allowed access to books, I read, and when I was denied such access, I wrote.

When I was first imprisoned, I had not yet finished high school. I was so eager to learn, and luckily, I had such good influences around me, such as another prison mate, Nur

---

43   See Appendix

Abdul Rabb, a great intellectual and a friend, who guided me through my early readings. He introduced me to the works of Najib Mahfouz, Ihsan Abdel Quddous and Hanna Mina. He also recommended that I read translated Russian novels, and I did.

But the more translated work I read, the more I wondered what it would be like to read such great literature in its original form. So I began studying translation, first from English to Arabic, then from Hebrew to Arabic. Soon enough, my translated articles began to appear in prison publications, written by hand and distributed secretly among prisoners. However, much of my work would be regularly confiscated during prison raids, never to be returned to me.

Reading allowed me to escape, in my mind, to a world beyond the prison walls, where there are no metal gates, no watchtowers and no sadistic prison guards, to places where people are equal and where possibilities are endless. Like most challenging feats in life, starting was so difficult. Despite the long hours of silence during my isolation, it was not easy to overcome that mental obstacle of allowing oneself to escape the hardship of life and delve into reading, but I did not stop trying.

I cannot explain why learning languages was not a struggle for me but rather a source of joy. Many of the languages I learned, I acquired directly from people who spoke them—fellow prisoners who studied and lived in foreign lands, but were now trapped in small prison cells, like the rest of us. I learned English, Hebrew, French, Russian and Spanish this way.

For 27 years, I had little else to do aside from reading, learning languages, translating and penning down my thoughts and analyses. By the time I was set free, I had learned 16 different languages. I must say that I was raised by my parents to be studious and to love learning. They spent much of their meagre income to provide me with whatever books I asked for that were available in bookstores. When I was arrested, I had acquired and read over 3,000 books.

As soon as I was arrested, I grasped the nature of the long fight awaiting me. It is the same fight faced by all prisoners before me and those who are left behind. The Israeli prison administration basically tries to break our spirit, to keep us isolated and uninformed, while we struggle to maintain a semblance of our humanity, to retain a sense of order within the most chaotic surroundings. But, for me, learning new languages—my way of reclaiming my identity as a Palestinian intellectual—did not happen by accident.

I first learned Hebrew in order to be able to communicate with the prison guards, to fight for and demand our rights in their own language, to understand their conversations, read their newspapers and appreciate how they think and reason. I would use whatever information I gathered to inform my fellow prisoners. When the prison guards found out that I was studying, and beginning to understand and communicate in Hebrew, they made sure not to speak while I was present. They would only whisper to each other.

But I did not stop there. I continued learning. English was relatively easy because it was the only foreign language we learned at school, so I had a basic idea about grammar. Then I fell in love with the Romance languages, French, Spanish, Italian and Romanian; I took up Russian and German. And, since I had nowhere else to be, I thought, why stop here? I began learning Turkish, then Persian and Ethiopian. When I finally acquired books in Latin, I took on that task, which was not an easy one, but most exciting. For me, learning Latin was like studying a code that helped me understand other languages more easily. My curiosity also drove me to explore ancient Greek, Berber, Syriac, and

Aramaic. It is fascinating how languages connect us to our past and to each other. It all moves in rational lines through time and space, to tell the collective story of humanity.

Whenever I was allowed visitation, I only requested books in various languages. It was my only demand. Just books. Friends and family outside prison would have lists of books I needed and, when they could not find them in Palestine, they would locate them elsewhere, often as far away as Italy and Russia. The Aramaic language was the most difficult to learn, and Amazigh, the Berber language, was frankly the most mystifying.

One major challenge for language learners in prison, like me, was being moved about between various prisons. I was arrested in Jenin, then moved to Jnaid, in Nablus, before making the rounds of all Israeli prisons, to finally land in the Naqab Prison in the desert. Leaving many of my books and dictionaries behind, and often forced to abandon my numerous notes, was extremely painful. Having to start all over again was tough for me, but it never stopped me from trying. But under such unfortunate circumstances, there were opportunities. In every new prison, I met comrades who spoke the languages that I was studying and were often desperate to put them into practice.

Access to books in prison is a constant demand for all prisoners. For me, it was the main thing that mattered. We endured many gruelling hunger strikes just to be allowed access to books and to be allowed the right to pursue our education. But, even then, I would wait weeks—sometimes, months—to acquire the books that I needed to further my studies and to help educate my fellow prisoners.

In the many years I spent in prison, I taught hundreds of comrades English and Hebrew.

I read for nearly eight hours every single day. I read books on history, politics and international relations.

I also read many books on psychology, media, economics, medicine and philosophy.

I was only allowed to pursue my education ten years after I was sentenced. As soon as I was permitted by the Israeli prison authority to join a university, I began taking classes at the Hebrew University,[44] where I obtained my Bachelor's degree in History and Political Science.

While in prison, I translated several books, including the biography of late Israeli president, Shimon Peres, and a book on Palestinian refugees. I also wrote a book of political analysis on the Gaza war, entitled: "The Unjust War 2008-2009." My resources were all based on Hebrew, English and Arabic newspapers and television broadcasts. I also translated 4,000 articles during my stay in Jnaid, Ramon and Bir al-Saba prisons.[45] During a prison raid, the guards confiscated all of my translated work. I lost everything. I had hoped to publish all the articles in a series of books when I was freed. Anticipating such a possibility, I attempted to send some of my work, at least my poetry and various reflections, home with my dad. But he stopped visiting me in later years because he had become too old and frail. I felt sorry for him as he had to endure much humiliation every time he visited me. I thought it was best that way. But then, I was left all alone for years.

Hungry for more education, as soon as I was set free, I obtained a Master's degree in Middle Eastern Studies from Al-Azhar University in Gaza. One day, I wish to establish a bilingual television station in both Hebrew and Russian, so that it can communicate the Palestinian message to Israeli

---

44   The Hebrew University is Israel's second-oldest university. It was established in 1918, 30 years before the creation of the State of Israel. Times Higher Education, accessed July 30, 2019, <https://www.timeshighereducation. com/world-university-rankings/hebrew-university-jerusalem>.

45   See Appendix.

society and challenge the Zionist propaganda. Russian immigrants to Israel have become a major constituency since the 1990s, and it is of vital importance that we engage them through our own media. Israel is a closed society and Israelis are constantly fed with their government's propaganda. We must disrupt this paradigm.

I try to stay in touch with all freed prisoners, and I know that many of them speak other languages, especially Hebrew. We are a talented people, and we define ourselves through our education and our intellect. We must not allow Israelis to define us in any way they want. Israel hates nothing more than educated Palestinians, which is unfortunate for them since we are a highly educated and achieving people.

Since I have been freed, I have had more opportunities to improve the languages that I learned. But I am not done; I plan to study more languages yet. I want to take the message of my people to every nation on this earth.

— *Hilal Mohammad Jaradat*

12

LOVE BEHIND BARS

Nael al-Barghouti and Iman Nafi'

NAEL Saleh al-Barghouti was born on October 24, 1957 in the village of Kobar, north of Ramallah in the West Bank. His five-member family includes his parents, his older brother, Omar, and his younger sister, Hanan. His father is Saleh al-Barghouti, a kindly man with strong religious beliefs, and his mother is a famed Palestinian poetess known as "Farha." They subsisted on farming, a tradition that runs deep in their family, forming an unbreakable bond between them and their land.

Nael was a student activist who took part in many protests against the Israeli occupation. He was arrested by Israeli soldiers at his family home in Kobar on April 4, 1978. After a long and harsh interrogation, he was sentenced to 112 years in prison for allegedly killing an Israeli occupation officer north of Ramallah. His brother, Omar, was also arrested, along with his cousin, Fakhri. Omar spent 26 years in prison, while Nael spent 34 years. Nael was released in a prisoner exchange between the Palestinian resistance and Israel in 2011.

Both brothers were detained, once more, shortly after their release. They remain in an Israeli prison until this day Iman Nimr Sarhan Nafi' was born in 1964 in the village of Ni'lin before her family moved to the city of

Ramallah, six years later. Like Nael's family, the Nafi's are also farmers. Iman studied nursing and joined a local hospital where she interacted with a mixed group of people, Palestinians and international medical staff. She describes her life in that period as "beautiful," especially as she drove her own car and had an exciting social life.

But such relative contentment was often interrupted by the Israeli occupation. Israeli soldiers raided the Nafi' family home many times, arresting and re-arresting Iman's brother. Happiness completely eluded Iman when her brother was shot in front of her during a protest in the city of Ramallah. While her political consciousness was formed at an early age, the wounding of her brother while peacefully protesting the Israeli occupation turned her life upside down.

Iman would soon join her people's resistance against Israeli occupation.

———

I WAS ONLY 17 YEARS OLD when, in 1981, I was first arrested by the Israeli army. But I was in prison for only a short period of time, since I was merely accused of organizing protests in my school, demanding freedom from Israel. Six years later, the stakes were much higher. On November 25, 1987, the soldiers came for me. They arrested me and, later, they arrested my mother and my brother. My mother, especially, suffered so much in jail since she was very ill.

I was held in Al-Maskobieh Detention Center[46] in Jerusalem, where I was subjected to very harsh interrogation as I was accused of planning to carry out an attack against an Israeli target in Yafa Street in Jerusalem. I remained strong despite the intense pressures, until I heard my mother's

---

46 See Appendix.

voice coming from one of the adjacent interrogation rooms. I tried to force my way through the soldiers while yelling: "My mother has nothing to do with this!"

They kept us both in one cell that was filled with rodents and cockroaches. My mother was very ill. Her high blood pressure required constant medical attention, none of which she received during her unfair imprisonment. She had difficulty in breathing, before she collapsed. I began screaming like a crazy person. Just seeing my poor mom lying on the dirty floor, unconscious, made me lose my mind. A while later, a soldier came with one of her blood pressure pills which they had confiscated. She was revived, but remained with me in the same dirty cell.

My mother was eventually released, but I was sentenced to 15 and a half years in prison. It hardly helped that the list of charges included an assault on a female prison guard. I needed to defend myself, as she had assaulted me and physically abused me while in detention. I spent ten of those years in prison and was released in 1997. Since then, I have dedicated my life to defending the rights of prisoners through my work with the Prisoners Club.[47] It would be years before I met, fell in love with and married Nael. Even though we did not live together for a long time, I feel as if he has been a part of me for my entire life.

Like me, Nael was only a high school student when he was arrested. But unlike me, his accusation was far more serious. In 1978, they charged him with the killing of an Israeli occupation soldier. He had spent more time in Israeli prisons than any other Palestinian prisoner. Although he was released in a prisoner exchange in 2011 after spending 34

---

47 The Palestinian Prisoners Club is a non-governmental organization that was established in 1993 to support political prisoners in Israeli occupation jails. "Palestinian Prisoners Club," Facebook, accessed July 29, 2019, <https://www.facebook.com/ppc1993/>.

uninterrupted years in Israeli jails, he was arrested again, along with 70 other freed prisoners. The Israeli government has decided to reinstate the 117 years sentence he was serving before they freed him. Every day, I pray for his freedom.

Two weeks after Nael was released, we began the wedding preparations, to be fully betrothed two months later. He was so desperate to claim a sense of normalcy in his life; he returned to farming his land in the village of Kobar near Ramallah, as soon as he was free. Sadly, the soldiers came back for him before he harvested what he had sown.

Nael's world had completely changed during his long imprisonment. His only sister was 12 years old when he was arrested. When he was released, she was a grandmother. But Nael did meet her eldest son, 'Inad, when 'Inad was arrested and imprisoned with his uncle. Nael met his nephew for the first time in prison.

Many of his loved ones passed away while Nael was in captivity. His father died in October 2004, and his mother followed, a year later. Despite every attempt to allow Nael to say goodbye to his dying mother, he was denied that basic human right as well.

I was so happy to be married to Nael. He, too, was thrilled. We both found love, and our life, for once, seemed to get back on track. Great festivities ensued. It was major news all over Palestine. Many freed prisoners with their families had joined our happy family in a traditional wedding that I would never forget. The Barghouti and Abu Haniyeh Nafi' clans were united in a rare moment of happiness.

Of course, we had to follow all traditional steps that usually precede the finalization of a marriage. Nael headed a delegation of respected men from Kobar who came to my original village, Ni'lin, officially asking for my hand. I cannot describe the feeling of joy in my family home on that day. I felt that our happiness was an act of defiance, of resistance, especially after being deprived of freedom for so long. We were separated by prison but united in our love for our homeland, and our faith in the justness of our struggle.

But, according to custom, someone other than Nael had to make the official request. Walid al-Haoudali was chosen for that task. Walid is an old comrade of Nael. They spent many years together in prison and were freed together. Walid stood and asked my uncle, Dheib, and my brother, Imad, for my hand. They immediately agreed, requesting only one Jordanian dinar as dowry. The amount was symbolic. It meant that my family was invested in Nael as a man, regardless of money or wealth. His reputation as a leader in our struggle for freedom was more than enough.

Then, Nael stood up and uttered these words:

As a freed prisoner, I consider my marriage to another freed prisoner a victory against prison, a challenge to those who deprived us of our freedom, and a triumph of the spirit of faith and hope. This joyous occasion is only the first step in unlocking the door of the life that still lies ahead of us. They denied us freedom, but didn't kill our determination to break our chains. Now, I can say that Iman and I will embark on a new journey, as we are about to start yet another family among this great nation. We pray to God that He completes our happiness and joy, and heals our wounds that have bled for too many years, leaving deep memories that will live with us forever. But these memories shall also serve as lessons that will strengthen our resolve to continue our march for freedom.

His passion and his strength were so palpable. He moved people. He moved me. I was immensely proud of him and excited about our life together.

Nael did not stop there. He spoke about those who died while he was in prison. He remembered his mother and his father. He spoke about our people in Gaza, their legendary struggle in their larger prison. He spoke about Palestinians in the diaspora and the need to strengthen our collective identity through celebrating our memories and our culture. "One day, all of us Palestinians shall be united together and that is the true celebration," he said. People nodded in agreement. Lots of tears fell on that day. Lots of hugs and kisses.

Happiness was real. I felt it.

Nael is a Palestinian hero. I have known of his heroism, his steadfastness and leadership in prison for many years. He is a special person. He belongs to a revolutionary school that is true and authentic and comes from the land itself. I have known so many details about his life, from what I have read and heard. When he came asking for my hand, I told my family that I agree without any hesitation. In him I saw a faithful life partner.

After we officiated the marriage, I thanked God for this precious gift. I was determined to build a happy family together, and do my best to compensate Nael for the 34 years he spent in prison. I knew the harsh conditions under which he was held as I had experienced some of that myself. I knew it would not be easy, but our love for each other, for Palestine and our faith in God would overcome all obstacles.

We lived together for 31 months before the Israeli army came to our house and re-arrested him. They gave no reason whatsoever as to why they reneged on the prisoner exchange agreement. He has been back in prison for years, and every hour of every day I think of him, of his suffering in prison and of the life that still awaits us.

From prison, he wrote this: "When a nation seeks its freedom, it will always prevail. The occupation will never succeed in planting defeat in our hearts, because we summon our courage from our faith in God and from the legacies of all the nations that sought and achieved their freedom and dignity."

Israel tries to impose restrictions on Nael in prison, to isolate him from others and from me, so that his messages to his people do not make it outside prison. But they will never succeed.

Nael is over 60 years old now, but the older he gets, the more rooted he becomes in his revolution, in his faith, in his land, in beautiful Kobar, in Palestine.

He is a Palestinian hero.

—Iman Nafi'

HUMANITARIAN HERO

Mohammed Khalil al-Halabi
—narrated by his father, Khalil al-Halabi

MOHAMMED Khalil al-Halabi was born on April 2, 1978. He is the second of seven brothers. The al-Halabi family was ethnically cleansed from the town of Al-Majdal in historic Palestine in 1948, to live in permanent exile ever since. Mohammed was born and raised in the Jabaliya refugee camp in the Gaza Strip.

In 2003, Mohammed earned a Master's degree in Civil Engineering from the Islamic University of Gaza. He is married with five children: Khalil, 15, 'Asem, 13, 'Amro, 9, Rital, 6, and Faris, 4.

In 2006, Mohammed became the Director of World Vision in Gaza, a US charity organization that, for 40 years, provided essential support to Palestinian communities in Jerusalem, the West Bank and Gaza, "serving the most poor and marginalized." A large portion of World Vision's budget is provided by the Australian government.[48]

The charity's work, like that of other international NGOs operating in the Gaza Strip, became critical after 2006,

---

48 "Inquiry Clears World Vision Gaza of Diverting Funds to Hamas," *The Guardian,* March 21, 2017, <https://www.theguardian.com/global-development/2017/mar/21/inquiry-clears-world-vision-gaza-of-diverting-funds-to-hamas>.

when Israel imposed a siege on the already impoverished region. Worsening an already difficult situation, several Israeli wars—starting in 2008—killed thousands of Palestinians in Gaza and destroyed much of the economic infrastructure of the Strip, leaving nearly half the population living under extreme poverty.[49]

It was then that Mohammed's work became essential for the survival of many, especially terminally ill cancer patients and families of fishermen and farmers who had lost their only source of income.

On June 15, 2016, Mohammed was arrested by Israeli occupation forces at the Beit Hanoun (Eretz) Crossing which separates besieged Gaza from Israel, in a joint operation carried out by the Shin Bet security service, the Israeli army and Israeli police. Since then, many have speculated that the real motives behind Mohammed's detention were to sever the last line of international support that has allowed Gaza to survive, despite the siege and war.

Coupled with the numerous Israeli-imposed restrictions on the UN refugee agency in Palestine, UNRWA, and other similar groups, Mohammed's case fits neatly into a larger trajectory of Israeli efforts to undermine international support for the Palestinian people.

To obtain a confession, Israel has subjected Mohammed to what the Palestinian Commission of Detainees and Ex-Detainees' Affairs refers to as "one of the longest trials in the history of the Palestinian captive movement."[50]

---

49   "UN: Poverty Worsening in Gaza," *Al Jazeera*, July 24, 2008, <https://www.aljazeera.com/news/middleeast/2008/07/2008724150311503436.html>.

50   According to the Commission of Detainees and Ex-Detainees Affairs website, the Commission "is the only legal and official heir of the ministry of detainees' affairs, which was established in 1998 upon a presidential decree. The commission was established upon a presidential decree on 29/5/2014 by President Mahmood Abbas, the president of the state of Palestine." CDA, Government of Palestine, accessed August 3, 2019, <http://cda.gov.ps/index.php/en/2018-03-12-10-54-51/definition-of-authority>.

———————◆———————

MOHAMMED'S ORDEAL BEGAN ON JUNE 15, 2016 at the Beit Hanoun (Eretz) Crossing. He was arrested by Israeli occupation soldiers on his way back from a World Vision meeting in Jerusalem. We only learned of his detention three days later. We were also told that he was being held in Askalan Prison.

My son experienced horrific torture while in Askalan. His interrogators accused him of funneling money to the resistance in Gaza. Absurdly, the sums of money he was accused of channeling to these Gaza groups exceeded the total budget of the Charity in the Strip. The whole story makes no sense.

Mohammed spent 52 days under constant and harrowing interrogation. From the very first day of detention, the Israeli intelligence officers placed a filthy bag over his head and hanged him from the ceiling for prolonged periods of time. They denied him sleep, and whenever they were done with their terrible deeds, they would throw him into an extremely tiny cell, barely large enough for one person to sit down, let alone sleep. He would be left there without a mattress and without a cover.

He was physically assaulted on numerous occasions. Each time, they would follow the same brutal routine: they slapped him, kicked him, especially in his genitals, and then strangled him until he felt that he was about to die. They would stop and resume a short while later. At times, they placed him in a small room and played extremely loud music until the pain in his ears became unbearable. In the summer, they would strip him naked, then blast him with flashes of warm air. They would repeat the same process in the winter, but with cold air, instead.

Mohammed's lawyer conveyed all of this to us in the most graphic details. My heart is broken for my son. All he was doing was trying to help needy people. He often spoke of empowering the downtrodden and disadvantaged in Gaza and, almost every day, he shared with me stories of the difference World Vision's work was making in the life of ordinary people. His time in prison, and all the physical torture he was forced to endure, have left him quite ill. Just the fact that they kept slamming him against the wall while shaking him repeatedly and violently, made him faint several times. But Israeli authorities refuse to let him see a doctor.

After they concluded their long and torturous interrogations, they transferred him to Nafha Prison, where he was paraded before a military court in Bir al-Saba'. At the time of writing these words, my son has endured 115 official and 60 non-official court sessions; the latter are meant to ensure that his treatment and torture are not placed on record. In fact, most of his trial was conducted in secrecy, despite international protests.[51]

The occupation wants Mohammed to admit to things he has not done. He said as much to the lawyer, that, no matter what they did to him, he will not assume responsibility for acts he did not commit. Despite the lies of the Israeli Ministry of Foreign Affairs that my Mohammed has admitted to diverting money to the resistance, my son officially pleaded not guilty to all charges against him in a district court trial in Bir Al-Saba' on February 2, 2017.[52] However, everyone

---

51   "Israel/OPT: 'Secret Trial' of Gaza Aid Worker Will Not Deliver Justice," Amnesty International, accessed August 3, 2019, <https://www.amnesty.org/en/latest/news/2016/08/israel-opt-secret-trial-of-gaza-aid-worker-will-not-deliver-justice/>.

52   "Palestinian NGO Worker Pleads Not Guilty to Helping Hamas," *The Times of Israel,* February 2, 2017, <https://www.timesofisrael.com/palestinian-ngo-worker-pleads-not-guilty-to-helping-hamas/>.

understands that the real reason behind all of this is that Israel wants to stop World Vision from operating in Gaza, a place that Israel wants to remain isolated, broken and pushed to its knees.

My son is an exceptional human being who has achieved so much in his young life, for his family and his people. He was featured in a UN campaign in 2014 as being one of the world's "humanitarian heroes."[53] World Vision itself awarded him "Humanitarian of the Year" for his tireless efforts to aid Gaza under these harsh conditions.

Aside from all the work that Mohammed did to help the poorest sector in Gaza society, much of his efforts focused on helping sick people, especially cancer patients who were denied access to proper health care and, often, to life-saving medicines. My son also focused much of his work on aiding the children who suffered numerous emotional and psychological scars as a result of the devastating Israeli wars.

Everyone knew my son, loved and respected him for the work he was doing, and all internal investigations, whether the one conducted by World Vision itself[54] or by the Australian government,[55] have absolved Mohammed from doing anything that runs contrary to the principles of charity work. But Israel refuses to set him free.

Now, Mohammed has been transferred once again, this time to Rimon Prison, where he is being held under extremely harsh conditions, still experiencing all sorts of torture and degradation. Israel has no evidence to indict

---

53 "Why I Am a Humanitarian," World Vision, accessed August 3, 2019, <https://www.wvi.org/world-humanitarian-day/article/why-i-am-humanitarian>.

54 "Statement by World Vision International CEO; Gaza Staff Member Pleads Not Guilty," World Vision, accessed August 3, 2019, <https://www.wvi.org/jerusalem-west-bank-gaza/pressrelease/statement-world-vision-international-ceo-gaza-staff-member>.

55 *The Guardian, supra.*n. 48.

my son, thus, it resorts to physically and psychologically tormenting him to get exactly what it wants to hear. By indicting Mohammed, the Israeli government wants to indict all international charities so that they completely suffocate Gaza and its heroic people.

We miss Mohammed. Gaza misses Mohammed. Every single day I try to do all I can to raise awareness of my son's cause. Thinking of him being mistreated in so demeaning a way eats me up on the inside. I want to hold him close to my chest and tell him how proud I am for all he has done for Gaza and the Palestinian people.

—Khalil al-Halabi

14

THE COHORT OF DEFIANCE

Khalida Jarrar

KHALIDA Jarrar was born in the city of Nablus in the northern West Bank on February 9, 1963. She currently resides in Ramallah with her husband, Ghassan, and two daughters, Suha and Yafa.

Jarrar has a Bachelor's degree in Business Administration and a Master's degree in Democracy and Human Rights from Birzeit University. She served as a director of Addameer Prisoners' Support and Human Rights Association from 1994 to 2006, when she was elected to the Palestinian Legislative Council (PLC)—the Palestinian Parliament. She now heads the PLC's Prisoners Commission, in addition to her role on the Palestinian National Committee for follow-up with the International Criminal Court.[56]

Jarrar's high profile as a Palestinian leader dedicated to exposing Israeli war crimes to international institutions has made her a target of frequent Israeli arrests and administrative detentions. She has been arrested three times, first in 1989, on the occasion of International Women's

---

56 "Khalida Jarrar," Addameer, Prisoner Support and Human Rights Association, accessed August 1, 2019, <http://www.addameer.org/prisoner/khalida-jarrar>.

Day. She spent a month in prison for taking part in the March 8 rally.

In 2015, she was detained in a pre-dawn raid by Israeli occupation soldiers, who stormed her house in Ramallah. Initially, she was held in administrative detention without trial, but, following an international outcry, Israeli authorities tried Jarrar in a military court, where 12 charges were made against her, based entirely on her political activities. Some of the charges included giving speeches, holding vigils and expressing support for Palestinian detainees and their families. She spent 15 months in prison.[57]

Jarrar was released in June 2016, only to be arrested again in July 2017, when she was also held under administrative detention. The Israeli raid on her home was particularly violent, as soldiers destroyed the main door of her house and confiscated various equipment, including an iPad and her mobile phone. She was interrogated at Ofer Prison before being transferred to HaSharon Prison, where many Palestinian female prisoners are held. She was released in February 2019, after spending nearly 20 months in prison.[58]

Instead of seeing prison as a forced confinement, Khalida has used it as an opportunity to educate and empower her fellow female prisoners. In fact, her achievements in prison changed the face of the Palestinian female prisoners' movement.

---

57   "Khalida Jarrar Freed—Palestinian Leftist Leader Calls for Action to Liberate Palestinian Prisoners," Samidoun, Palestinian Prisoner Solidarity Network, accessed August 1, 2019, <https://samidoun.net/2016/06/khalida-jarrar-freed-palestinian-leftist-leader-calls-for-action-to-liberate-palestinian-prisoners/>.

58   *Addameer, supra* n. 56.

FEMALE PRISONERS IN ISRAELI PRISONS are treated somewhat differently than males, not only in terms of the nature of the violations committed against them, but also in the degree of their isolation. Since there are far fewer female prisoners than males, it is easier for Israeli prison authorities to isolate them completely from the rest of the world. Moreover, there are only a few women prisoners with university degrees; the level of education among these women is alarmingly low.

I was already aware of these facts when I was detained by Israel in 2015, spending most of my detention in HaSharon Prison. Therefore, I decided to make it my mission to focus on the issue of education for women who were denied the opportunity to finish school, whether as children or those who were denied such a right due to difficult social conditions. The idea quickly occupied my mind: if I could only help a few women achieve their high school diplomas, I would have made good use of my time in detention. These diplomas would allow them to pursue university degrees as soon as they were able to and, eventually, achieve a level of economic independence. More importantly, armed with a strong education, these women could contribute even more to the empowerment of Palestinian communities.

But there are plenty of obstacles facing all prisoners, especially women. Israeli prison authorities place numerous restrictions on prisoners who want to pursue formal education. Even when the Israel Prison Service (IPS)[59] agrees, in principle, to grant such a right, they ensure that all practical conditions required to facilitate the work are missing, including the availability of classrooms, blackboards, school supplies and qualified teachers.

The latter obstacle, however, was overcome by the fact that I have a Master's degree, which qualifies me from

---

59 Israel Prison Service (IPS) is the national prison authority in Israel.

the viewpoint of the Palestinian Ministry of Education to serve as a teacher and to supervise final high school exams, known as Tawjihi. Just seeing the excitement on the faces of the girls when I floated the idea by them inspired me to take on the daunting task, the first such initiative in the history of Palestinian women prisoners in Israeli jails.

I began by contacting the Ministry of Education[60] in order to fully understand their rules and expectations, and how they would apply to female prisoners who want to study for their final exams. My first cohort of students consisted of five women, who so giddily took on the challenge.

At that early stage, the prison administration was not fully aware of the nature of our "operation," so their restrictions were merely technical and administrative. The experience was, in fact, new to all of us, especially to me. I must admit that I may have exaggerated my expectations in my attempt to ensure a high degree of academic professionalism in conducting my classes and the final exam. I just wanted to make sure that I did not, in any way, violate my principles, because I truly wanted the girls to earn their certificates and expect more of themselves.

We had few school supplies. In fact, each class had to share a single textbook that was left by Palestinian child prisoners before they were transferred by IPS to another facility. We copied the few textbooks by hand; this way, several students were able to follow the lessons at the same time. My students studied hard. A single class would, at times, extend to several hours, which meant that they would willingly lose their only break for the day when they were allowed to leave their cells. We had so much to cover and so little time. In the end, five students took the exam, the

---

60   The Ministry of Education is part of the Palestinian Authority in Ramallah.

results of which were sent to the Ministry of Education to be confirmed. Weeks later, the results came back. Two of the students passed.

It was an extraordinary moment. The news that two students had earned their certificates while in prison spread quickly among all the prisoners, their families, and organizations that champion detainees' rights. The girls celebrated the news, and all of their comrades felt truly happy for them. In no time, we mobilized again, getting ready to produce yet another cohort of graduates. However, the more media attention our achievement garnered, the more worried the Israeli prison authorities became. I was not at all surprised that the IPS decided to make it difficult for the second group, also consisting of five students, to go through the same experience.

It was a real battle, but we had every intention of fighting it to the end, no matter the pressure. The prison administration informed me officially that I was no longer allowed to teach the prisoners. They harassed me repeatedly, threatening to send me to solitary confinement. But I know international law well, and I repeatedly confronted the Israelis with the fact that I understood the rights of the prisoners and had no plans to back down. Despite all of this, I managed to teach the second group of girls, preparing the exams myself, in coordination with the Ministry of Education. This time, all five students who took the exam passed. It was a great triumph.

After what we achieved, I realized that there is a need to institutionalize the educational experience for female prisoners, and not to tie it to me or to any single person. For this to succeed in the long term, it needed to be a collective effort, a mission to be championed by every group of women in prison, for years to come. I placed much of my focus on training qualified female prisoners, by getting them involved in teaching and by familiarizing them with administrative work required by the Ministry of Education. I set up the apparatus to ensure a smooth transition for the third group of graduates, as I was anticipating my imminent release.

I was freed in June 2016. Although I returned to my regular life and professional work, I never ceased thinking about my comrades in prison, their daily struggles and challenges, especially those who were keen on getting the education that they need and deserve. I was thrilled when I learned that two female prisoners took on the final exams after I left, and successfully graduated. I felt as happy as I did when I was freed and reunited with my family. I was also relieved to learn that the system I put in place before my release was working. This gave me much hope for the future.

In July 2017, the Israeli military arrested me again, this time for 20 months. I returned to the same HaSharon Prison. There were many more female prisoners than before. Immediately, with the help of other qualified prisoners, we began preparing for the fourth group to graduate. This time, nine female prisoners were studying for the exam. There were more volunteer teachers and administrators. The prison had suddenly bloomed, turning to a place of learning and empowerment.

The prison administration went crazy! They accused me of incitement and began a series of retaliatory measures to shut down the whole schooling process. We accepted the challenge. When they closed our classroom, we went on strike. When they confiscated our pens and pencils, we used crayons instead. When they hauled away our blackboard, we unhooked a window and wrote on it. We smuggled it from one room to another, during the times that we had designated for learning. The prison guards tried every trick in the book to prevent us from our right to education. To show our determination to defeat the prison authorities, we named the fourth group "The Cohort of Defiance." In the end, our will proved mightier than their injustice. We completed the entire process. All the girls who took the final exam passed with flying colors.

I cannot describe to you in mere words how we felt during those days. It was a huge victory. We decorated the prison walls and celebrated. We were all happy, smiling and jubilant because of what we managed to achieve together, when we stood united against the unfair rules of Israel and its prison administration. The news spread beyond the prison walls and celebrations were held by the families of the graduates throughout Palestine.

The fifth group was the crowning of that collective achievement. It was the sweet reward following months of struggle and hardship that we had endured, while insisting on our right to education. Seven more students are now studying for the final exam, in the hope of joining the other 18 female graduates who obtained their certificates since the first experience commenced in 2015.

The aspirations of female prisoners evolved, as they felt truly capable and empowered by the education they had received, especially as they had endured so much to obtain what should be a basic human right for all. Those who have obtained their Tawjihi certificates are ready to progress to a higher level of education. However, since the Ministry of Education is not yet prepared for this step, the prisoners are creating temporary alternatives.

Since I have a Master's degree in Democracy and Human Rights, and also have lengthy experience in this field through my work with Addameer and the PLC, among other institutions, I offered my students a training course in International and Humanitarian Law. To teach the course, I managed to bring into prison some of the most important and relevant texts pertaining to international treaties on human rights, including the Arabic translations of all four Geneva Conventions. Some of these documents were brought in by the Red Cross, others by family members who came to visit me in prison.

Forty-nine female prisoners participated in the course, which was divided into several periods, each consisting of two months. At the end of the course, the participants received certificates for having completed 36 hours of training in International and Humanitarian Law, the results of which were confirmed by several Palestinian ministries. While we celebrated in prison, a large ceremony sponsored by the Ministry of Prisoners' Affairs was held outside, where the families and some of the freed prisoners attended, amid a huge celebration.

In the end, we did more than fashion hope out of despair. We also evolved in our narrative, in the way we perceive ourselves, the prison and the prison guards. We defeated any lingering sense of inferiority and turned the walls of prison into an opportunity. When I saw the beautiful smiles on the faces of my students who completed their high school education in prison, I felt that my mission has been accomplished.

Hope in prison is like a flower that grows out of a stone. For us Palestinians, education is our greatest weapon. With it, we will always be victorious.

—*Khalida Jarrar*

15

The pigeons fly,
the pigeons come down...
Prepare a place for me to rest.
I love you unto weariness,
your morning is fruit for songs
and this evening is precious gold
the pigeons fly
the pigeons come down...
My love, I fear the silence of your hands
I am for my lover I am. And my lover is for his
*   wandering star*
Sleep my love
on you my hair braids, peace be with you...
the pigeons fly
the pigeons come down...
                                              —Mahmoud Darwish

"I CANNOT LOSE MY HUSBAND"

Mohammad Adeeb al-Qiq
—narrated by his wife, Fayha' Shalash

MOHAMMAD *Adeeb al-Qiq is a Palestinian journalist from the town of Dura, south of Hebron in the West Bank. He now lives with his family in Birzeit, north of Ramallah. He was born on April 21, 1982. He is the fifth of seven siblings: five brothers and two sisters. Al-Qiq is married to a fellow journalist, Fayha' Shalash. Together they have three children: Islam, seven, Lour, four, and five-month-old Leya.*

Al-Qiq has a Master's degree in Modern Arabic Studies from Birzeit University. He worked as a correspondent with the Saudi news network, Al-Majd, covering the Occupied West Bank. His television reports on the Israeli army's execution of alleged Palestinian attackers, during what was known as the Al-Quds Uprising,[61] received much attention throughout the Middle East and earned al-Qiq much admiration among Palestinians.

---

61 "In October 2015, Israel's actions at Al-Aqsa Mosque compound triggered a wave of Palestinian anger, which led to the Al-Quds Uprising." "Is a Third Palestinian Intifada Imminent?," *Al Jazeera,* October 13, 2015, <https://www.aljazeera.com/programmes/insidestory/2015/10/palestinian-intifada-imminent-151013164158529.html>.

As a result of his popular work, a large contingent from the Israeli army paid him a late-night visit, an event that almost ended his life.

———————◆———————

It was on Saturday, November 21, 2015, a month and a half after the start of the Al-Quds Uprising, that Israeli soldiers raided our house. There were too many, accompanied by armoured vehicles and army jeeps. The soldiers dynamited the main door of our humble home before they all rushed inside, in the most terrifying scene one could ever imagine. We all huddled together in panic. In the end, they arrested my husband, Mohammad, and confiscated all digital devices, papers and documents.

This was the fourth time that Mohammad was arrested. His first arrest was in 2003, when he was held for a month; then, again, in 2004, for 13 months. In 2008, he was sentenced by an Israeli court to 16 months in prison, for his political activities and involvement in the Birzeit University Student Council.

When Mohammad was arrested the fourth time, our two children were mostly unaware of what was happening to their dad. Islam was spared the painful experience of seeing his father on the ground, being handcuffed and blindfolded. But when he woke up in the morning and saw the broken glass and smashed door, he inquired about what had happened to the house. When I told him that his father was taken by soldiers, his lips quivered and his face conveyed emotions of fear and sadness that no child should ever experience.

Lour was only one year old at the time. As the soldiers were arresting her father, she kept hugging him and playfully touching his cheeks.

Mohammad was then taken to the infamous Al-Jalameh Detention Center[62] for interrogation. He was not allowed to see a lawyer; thus, we had no news from him whatsoever. We had no other option but to wait and pray. His detention was extended several times, but still without any information on his well-being. In mid-December, I was browsing the Internet when I discovered through the news that my husband had been on a hunger strike for 11 days. It meant that he had started his strike four days after his initial detention.

I immediately phoned the Prisoners' Club. By sheer chance, a lawyer who saw Mohammad in court was present. He told me that Mohammad was tried in a closed court session, meaning that neither family nor legal counsel was present or even informed of the trial. As he was taken back to his cell, he ran into the Palestinian lawyer and managed to shout these words before he was hurriedly rushed outside the court: "I am prisoner Mohammad al-Qiq. Tell my family and the media that I am on an open hunger strike. I am currently held at Al-Jalameh."

When I heard this, I became very scared. We have never experienced this as a family. I did not fully fathom the impact of such a decision on our family, but more importantly, on Mohammad himself. It was then that my journey began, fighting for my husband's freedom. For months, I pursued every human rights group that could help me obtain any information about Mohammad's mental and physical health. The Israelis had nothing against Mohammad, aside from the fact that he was a journalist and, according to their twisted logic, they equated that with being a terrorist. They kept him in interrogation for 26 days, despite his deteriorating health. When he began throwing up blood and could no longer stand on his own, he was transferred to the Ramleh Prison Hospital.

---

62   See Appendix.

Mohammad became even more determined to carry on with his hunger strike when the Israeli court sentenced him to six months of administrative detention[63]—which means that they could not support their accusations against my husband with any tangible evidence, but they still refused to free him. The administrative detention order was renewable for up to three years. For me, it was a race against time as I needed to convey to the world that my husband was an innocent man, and that his only wish was to return to his home and children, and that journalism is not a crime. But I also feared that it might be too late, that my husband could die before that message resonated throughout Palestine and the world.

As his health continued to worsen, he was taken to the Afouleh Hospital[64], where they tried to force him to eat. He refused. When they tried to feed him through an I.V., he tore the needle out of his arm and threw it on the ground. I know my husband. For him, life without freedom is just not worth living.

A month into his hunger strike, Mohammad began throwing up yellow bile and blood. The pain in his gut and joints and the chronic headaches were unbearable. Despite all of this, they still tied him to his hospital bed. His right arm and both feet were secured with heavy shackles to the four corners of the bed. He was left like this the entire time.

I felt that Mohammad was going to die. My fear was compounded for my captive husband and for our children. I tried to explain to my son that his father was refusing food so

---

63 According to Addameer, "administrative detention is a procedure that allows the Israeli military to hold prisoners indefinitely on secret information without charging them or allowing them to stand trial." Addameer, accessed August 3, 2019, <http://www.addameer.org/israeli_military_judicial_system/administrative_detention>.

64 See Appendix.

that he could obtain his freedom. Islam kept saying: "When I grow up, I will hit the occupation." Lour missed her dad, but did not understand anything. As I fought for their dad's freedom, I had no other option but to be away from them for long periods of time. Our little family was broken up.

On February 4, 2016, Mohammad entered his 77th day of hunger strike. Under popular and international pressure, but mainly because of Mohammad's own unbendable will, the Israeli occupation was forced to halt the administrative detention order. However, for Mohammad, that was just not enough. He carried on with his strike for weeks after that decision.

I chose not to visit my husband while he was in prison. It was the most difficult decision I have ever had to make, staying away from the man I love, the father of my children. But I knew that if he saw me or the kids, he could become too emotional, or worse, he could physically break down even further. I remained committed to this decision up to the end.

At one point, I thought to myself: "Mohammad will never come back, and he will die in prison." As he reached the 80th day of his hunger strike, his body began to go into spasms. I learned later that these involuntary spasms were extremely painful. Each time they took place, he recited the Shahada—"There is No God but Allah and Mohammad is His Prophet"—in anticipation of his death. Many times, he felt that death was forthcoming.

Mohammad was so close to his kids. He loved them with all of his heart and tried to spend as much time with them as he could. Often, he would carry both of them for a long time while walking around the house or the neighbourhood. As his death became a possibility, I wondered what I would say to the kids, how I would answer their questions as they grew up without a father, and how I would carry on without him.

Being aware of what seemed to be his inevitable death, Mohammad wrote his last will and testament. I first learned about it while watching Al-Jazeera television. Suddenly, my whole world collapsed before my eyes. Mohammad's will read:

> I would like to see my wife and children, Islam and Lour before I die. I just want to be sure that they are okay. I would also like the final prayer on my body to be conducted inside the Durra Mosque. Please bury me inside the grave of my mother, so that she can hold me the way she did when I was still a child. If that is not feasible, please bury me as close to her as possible. Please don't overburden the mourners with a long ceremony where they stand the whole day on their feet, and just limit it to the hours between the 'Asr prayer (in the afternoon) and the 'Isha prayer (at night).

I tried to ignore his will and, instead, focused on the few words he had conveyed to me earlier through a lawyer. These words kept me composed and gave me the hope I needed to stay strong and fighting: "Have faith in God, my beloved. Rest assured that we will drink coffee together on our balcony again, as we have done every morning."

Throughout his hunger strike, the children's photos remained by Mohammad's hospital bed. "Do my kids remember me?" he used to ask whoever visited him. He thought of us always, and us of him. At the end of his hunger strike, his body was reduced to skin and bones. His athletic build collapsed upon itself, but his spirit continued to soar, as if the weaker he felt physically, the stronger his will had become.

In the end, his determination proved stronger than the injustice of his tormentors. On February 26, 2016, it was announced that an agreement was reached between the Palestinian prisoners committee, representing Mohammad, and the Israeli prison administration. My husband was to be released on May 21 of the same year, nearly three months after ending his hunger strike. While recovering at the Afouleh Prison, Mohammad was assaulted by an extremist Jewish settler, so he was transferred to the Ramleh Prison, then to Nafha, until he finished his six-month term.

Mohammad seized his freedom after 94 days on hunger strike. He proved to the world that he was not a terrorist as the Israelis claimed, and that all he had endured was simply for conveying the suffering of his people to the world. Because of his unrelenting resistance, Israeli military authorities were forced to withdraw all accusations against him.

Mohammad's imprisonment remains a painful memory, but also a great victory for Palestinians everywhere. Mohammad entered prison weighing 99 kilograms (218 pounds), and when he ended his strike, he was only 45 kilograms (99 pounds). When I came to visit him with our children one week after the end of his strike, I could not recognize him. I thought I had entered the wrong room, but when I drew closer, I saw his kind, loving eyes, so I held him and I cried. Islam seemed scared as he looked at his father lying on the bed like a skeleton.

Mohammad was released on the agreed upon date, but he was re-arrested eight months later. He immediately began another hunger strike that lasted for 33 days. The kids were even more attached to him now, as they had grown older and more aware of his presence. I had to pull Islam out of his kindergarten. I could not leave him alone. When all the children graduated with colourful certificates, Islam did not get one. He kept asking me why, and I told him that it was not his fault, but because it was not possible for him to finish his class due to his father's imprisonment. I saw him holding back his tears. He felt sad for a long time.

Mohammed is currently free, but my kids still speak about prison. Islam is worried that his father could be arrested again at night. I tell him not to worry, but I am terrified of that possibility myself.

I long for a day where I no longer worry that I may lose my husband.

—Fayha' Shalash

16

"THEY HELD A FUNERAL FOR ME"

Azmi Ahmad Mansour

AZMI Ahmad Rasheed Mansour was born on September 27, 1950 in Kufr Kanna in the lower Galilee, Occupied Palestine. He was arrested on March 17, 1968. As soon as he turned 18, he was convicted to a life sentence with labor in Jenin Prison. Azmi was released in a prisoners' exchange deal on May 20, 1985 after 18 years of imprisonment. He now lives in Amman, where he is married to a Palestinian lady, Nabila, originally from Jaffa.

———————

AT 17 YEARS OF AGE, I witnessed the Naksa[65] of 1967, a bitter war of displacement. I saw the droves of refugees and dead bodies. My family had to escape from Jenin to Irbid in Jordan. On the way, I saw many displaced families suffering

---

65 "Naksa literally means 'setback' or 'relapse' and refers to the second Nakba—the expulsion of Palestinians from the West Bank, East Jerusalem and Gaza during the 1967 war. It also marks the beginning of Israel's illegal military occupation of these territories." "From the 1948 Nakba to the 1967 Naksa," *Badil Occasional Bulletin No. 18,* June 2004, <http://www.badil.org/phocadownloadpap/Badil_docs/bulletins-and-briefs/Bulletin-18.pdf>.

in the desert. These images were enough to compel me to join the Resistance and defend my country.

In one Resistance operation, I was hit by two bullets and shrapnel in the same foot, after which I was arrested, on March 17, 1968. I was held in Jenin Prison and convicted to a life sentence with labor. I was tortured and did not receive medical care for my injuries. Instead, I was thrown into a cell and suffered from my wounds for a long time. After conviction, I was transferred to Askalan Prison.

My family thought I had died, as my friends who had carried out the operation with me believed that I had, and told them so. They held a funeral for me. I managed to smuggle a letter to my grandfather in Jordan and they could not believe I was alive. When they received the letter, they began to compare the writing with that in my school books, and my grandfather came to visit me. But I was in solitary confinement, so they would not let him see me. The following month, he was able to bring my grandmother and visit me. A year later, my mother was able to see me. It was a difficult visit, laden with longing and tears, but I tried as hard as I could to console her, to give her hope that I would be out soon.

Askalan Prison was created to torture those who had resisted. When a new prisoner arrived, he was made to walk between two rows of soldiers and officers, who beat him with sticks and hoses. Then, his hair, beard and moustache were shaved. We tried to grow our moustaches in order to annoy them, and to resist even in this small way.

We could not live like this, and were forced to declare a hunger strike. We had to break the martial laws and barbaric treatment against us. The first strike lasted a week, but our demands were not met, so we renewed it for 21 days, still with no fulfillment of all our demands. I took part in all subsequent strikes, the longest of which lasted 45 days. The strikes usually achieved some of our demands, but mostly, the Israeli prison service would promise us, then renege on its promises. They were bargaining with our basic rights to food, drink and sleep, and 25 people were being crammed into a 25 square meter (270 square foot) room, forced to sleep on the floor, with no consideration for health or human conditions.

During our first hunger strike, we fought for improvement of our food. Breakfast was composed of half a boiled egg, a spoon of butter and jam, a few olives, and two or three pieces of bread, at best. Lunch was a tasteless and colorless soup, and dinner was very similar to breakfast. This was served to about 450 prisoners, most of whom were on long sentences.

The decision to go on hunger strike was due to this suffering and unmet demands, initiated with an agreement among the leaders of the prisoners inside the prison. The date of the strike was decided and the lawyers and families of prisoners were informed. At the start, we would refuse to have food brought into our rooms; they would be searched and all the food would be removed. Then, the strike would begin in stages; the strongest and sturdiest prisoners would go first; then those of medium build, and, finally, those with frail health. The first day is always difficult, following which the body begins to adjust. We always keep salt at hand, for fear of infection of the stomach and intestines due to the long fast, and we only drink water. Thus, we only consumed water and salt on our strikes.

In ten days, forced feeding of the striking prisoners would begin. The prison officials would first put fruit in front of us to tempt us, but we would refuse. Then, they would try to force feed us through tubes inserted into the nose or mouth, carrying highly salted milk. This is an excruciating procedure. Due to its immense dangers on the life and health of prisoners, it was stopped, and they were forced to drink a glass of very salty milk. These prisoners were still considered to be on strike.

As the days passed with the ongoing strike, our vision would deteriorate and our bodies would grow very weak. During one strike, when we were not achieving anything, we revolted, threw our blankets outside our cells and set fire to them. As punishment, the prison guards came into our cells and beat us violently, breaking many prisoners' limbs.

Askalan Prison has held some of the most important figures of the Palestinian Resistance. There, I met Samir al-Quntar, Omar Kassim, Mustafa Khmeis, and many leaders of the front line of the revolution. The demands that we achieved in this prison would be propagated to other prisons, while the reverse was not always true.

Despite the hardship, we would take part in sports, read during the day and in the evenings, we would have cultural lectures. We also taught prisoners who could not read, and improved the education of those who could. Some prisoners studied languages, depending on the humble books or knowledge of other prisoners, and we carried this lifelong learning habit with us after our release.

Life in prison, especially in solitary confinement, leads you to seek strange friendships: you may befriend an ant or a cockroach, or any insect. I would observe their movements and digging, trying to find solace and distraction in anything so I would remain steadfast in the face of the prison administration.

I was held in prison for 18 years, 16 and a half of them in Askalan, then in Ramleh Prison, then in Jneid Prison[66] in Nablus, where I was finally released in a prisoners' exchange deal on May 20, 1985, the first day of Ramadan. We knew

---

66 See Appendix.

about this for a while beforehand when our families visited us, so we were prepared. Priority was given to prisoners with long sentences; that included me. The Red Cross came and called out our names, separated us from the others and gave us a change of clothes. We said goodbye to our fellow prisoners. We were then flown from Lydda (Ben Gurion) Airport to Switzerland, where the exchange took place and 1120 prisoners were released, most of whom with lengthy sentences. We wished our fellow prisoners, who were left behind, were also with us.

—Azmi Ahmad Mansour

17

THE BOY FROM HARIS

Ali Yasin Shamlawi
—Narrated by his Mother, N'imeh Shamlawi

ON MARCH 17, 2013, Ali Yassin Shamlawi was detained with four other Palestinian teenagers from the village of Haris, near the city of Salfit in the central region of the Occupied West Bank. Ali, along with Mohammad Klaib, Tamer Sof, Ammar Sof and Mohammad Suleiman, became known as the "Haris boys" as their arrest, torture and trial captured national and international attention, especially as they spent three years in detention, later to be tried and sentenced as adults.

Ali was only 16 when Israeli soldiers detained him, along with the other boys. The five were accused of throwing rocks at a vehicle belonging to Israeli settlers from Ariel, a Jewish-only settlement built illegally on ethnically cleansed Palestinian land. The Israeli driver claimed that the boys threw rocks at the vehicle, causing a car accident that resulted in the injury of an Israeli child, Adele Biton.

The Israeli military court discounted the testimony of Palestinian witnesses and only upheld the account of the Jewish settlers. The "Haris boys" maintain their innocence to this day. Ali told the human rights organization, Defense of Children International-Palestine, that he only confessed to throwing stones under torture and during a prolonged period of solitary confinement.[67]

Ali was initially held in al-Jalameh, a notorious Israeli military detention center near the city of Haifa, built atop the ruins of a Palestinian village that was depopulated and destroyed in 1948. There, Ali was tortured for 22 days. Despite being a minor at the time, Ali was not allowed to communicate with anyone, not even a lawyer, except for his Israeli interrogators. After the forced confession, Ali, along with the other "Haris boys," faced a trial consisting of more than 60 different sessions, where he was finally sentenced to 15 years in prison. Throughout the duration of the trial, he was held in Megiddo Prison[68] *for two years, before he was moved to the Ramon Prison*[69] *and finally to the Naqab (Negev) Desert Prison, where he is currently serving his long sentence.*

Soon after his arrival, Ali signed up for classes at Al-Quds Open University,[70] *where he is now pursuing a bachelor's degree.*

Ali was only allowed family visitation after six months following his initial imprisonment.

———————◆———————

67 "'Haris Boys' Sentenced to 15 Years despite Fair Trial Violations," Defense for Children International, accessed August 3, 2019, <https://www.dci-palestine.org/_haris_boys_sentenced_to_15_years_despite_fair_trial_violations>.

68 See Appendix.

69 See Appendix.

70 Al-Quds Open University is an independent public university founded in 1985, in Amman, Jordan. It launched its first campus in Palestine in 1991. International Association of Universities, accessed August 3, 2019, <https://whed.net/detail_institution.php?Jjo2MF0tU0RVCmAK>.

I TOOK MY SEAT ON THE BUS NEXT TO MY HUSBAND. It was the first time I was allowed to see my son, Ali, six months after his arrest. The bus belonged to the Red Cross, and all the passengers were families like us from the Salfit region in the West Bank.

The journey began at 6:30 in the morning. We arrived at the Qalqilya military checkpoint about 45 minutes later. However, we were held at the checkpoint for nearly two and a half hours. We were all thoroughly searched and humiliated. The soldiers yelled at us, insulted us with profane language, delayed us for no reason and then searched us, all over again. We remained composed, because every parent on that bus was consumed with the hope of seeing their child. Nothing but Ali was on my mind. I tried to imagine the moment I would see him. What should I say? What if I break into tears? How can I leave without him?

When I saw him at the Salem military court a few weeks after his initial arrest, in March 2013, I wanted to cry, to scream. My heart sank when they brought him in—my son, my 16-year-old boy and the youngest and most spoiled of all of my children. He stood there, bewildered, handcuffed and shackled. He looked scared. Exhausted. He had lost so much weight. I was not allowed to talk to him, to touch him, to hug him. Still, I held my tears, along with that muted scream that I could only let out when I returned home. I gestured to him from afar and shouted "Stay strong, son. God is with us!"

Our bus journey lasted another hour before we reached the Megiddo prison, where Ali was held briefly after the end of his torture and interrogation. We were dropped at a large, caged space with a massive electric gate. We waited there for two more hours. I had in my purse some money to deposit in his prison account so that he could purchase a few necessities from the prison's canteen. I also had a duffle bag with a few items of clothing that had to adhere to the specific prison instructions of being of a certain color and fabric.

The soldiers then divided us into groups. We were listed in the first group that was called to enter. First we had to be corralled before more electronic gates and subjected to further physical searches. Finally, we arrived at a rectangular visitors' hall with wooden chairs lined up before a wall. The separation wall was made of cement, upon which massive slabs of thick, impenetrable glass were erected. By each chair there was a phone handset, and a corresponding handset on the other side. We waited for another 15 minutes. Against one side of the wall, families, mothers and fathers stood, as they fought their tears, some beseeching God for mercy and waiting desperately for the doors on the other side to open.

Then, he arrived. Ali. My sweet, sweet boy. He had this excited look on his face, his eyes giddily searching the crowd on the other side of the glass wall for us. You could see the joy on his face when he saw me with his dad. I was so eager to hug my child, I would have broken the glass and held him in my arms, to never leave without him. I knew that my embrace would wash away the months of torture, humiliation and fatigue. I pitied him. I pitied myself and my husband, as the three of us stood there in a sea of emotion, tears, eager to break free, and the determination to remain strong and steadfast.

I quickly grabbed the phone handle. "Darling. Habibi. How are you?" I started. But his voice arrived faint and hardly audible. I could barely hear him. I kept asking him to raise his voice, to repeat what he had said. His father took the phone from me and began instructing Ali: "Stay strong, my son. Now you are a man. Circumstances forced you to grow older beyond your years, and you must meet the challenges of life head-on." Ali tried to assure us that he was fine; he said that he had many friends, and that comrades in prison were looking after him. We told him how proud of him we were, that all of Haris, all of Salfit, in fact, all of Palestine was proud of him. He asked us about his friends at school, his teachers and neighbors as, for a fleeting moment, he wanted to feel that everything was just fine. Every time he would mention the name of any of his four brothers, his eyes would tear up. But when he mentioned his only sister, to whom he was very close, he paused. Tears rolled down his face. "Tell her I love her," he said.

We spent 45 minutes with him. It was not long enough. It was so difficult for me to walk away. I felt that my heart was being ripped out of my chest. Who will take care of my son for the next 15 years? Who will comfort him during his moments of pain? Who will look after him when he is sick? Then I broke down, crying. I had done so well till that moment, but as the soldiers dragged him back to his cell, all of my strength suddenly vanished. I felt as if my heart had broken into a thousand pieces.

I count the days to see him free once more. Whenever a prison comrade of his is freed, I rush with my husband to visit him and seek news of Ali. "You must be proud of your son," they always tell us. "You raised a kind and polite son," they say. When Ali was first arrested, he was a child. Others looked after him. It has been nearly six years. Now, he looks after and comforts others. My boy is now a man, and a good-hearted one. He is also keeping up with his studies. He should graduate from university soon. When he fully serves his sentence, he will be 31 years old.

Ali was unjustly imprisoned. All the "Haris boys" were.

I think of my little boy every waking hour.

—*N'imeh Shamlawi*

18

THE "BOSTA" IS AN IRON CAGE

Khadija Ahmad Ibrahim Khweis

KHADIJA Khweis was born on August 27, 1977 in the small town of At-Tur on the Mount of Olives, adjacent to the Old City of Occupied East Jerusalem (Al-Quds). She is married, with three girls and two boys.

In 2014, Khadija joined al-Murabitat (Steadfast Women), a civil society organization composed mostly of Jerusalemite women. They have taken on the role of defending Al-Aqsa Mosque and other holy shrines in the occupied Palestinian city against Israeli army and police attacks and Jewish settlers' raids. Their weapons are protests, civil disobedience tactics and prolonged vigils. They are all aimed at organizing the community and creating awareness of the Israeli strategy to Judaize Jerusalem and target its Muslim and Christian Arab inhabitants.[71] Members of al-Murabitat, which is outlawed by Israel, often pay a heavy price for their ongoing protests.

---

71 For Israel, erasing Palestine and writing the Palestinian people out of the history of their own homeland have always been a strategic endeavor. The Israeli Zionist campaign to rename Palestinian places, destroy Palestinian heritage sites, claim Palestinian culture, undermine the Arabic language and erase cultural contributions of the Palestinian people has continued for over 70 years.

Khadija has been detained 18 times, for periods ranging from several days to several weeks. At times, and for years on end, she was placed under house arrest, barred from entering the Old City, the West Bank and denied freedom of movement. However, at the end of each sentence, she would immediately resume her place at the frontlines of popular resistance in Al-Quds.

The list of Israeli accusations against her is quite long, but they mostly fall into a single category: obstructing the activities of Israeli troops and armed settlers in Occupied Jerusalem. For her, no punishment was as painful as being denied the right to visit her beloved Al-Aqsa.

Khadija was once detained for over three weeks, September 6-28, 2017. The most difficult part of that imprisonment was the bosta, the name given to the Israeli inter-prison transfer vehicle.

Despite the numerous risks, Khadija, like hundreds of Jerusalem women, remains steadfast.

———————

I WAS SUFFOCATING. I could hear the other prisoners in their individual, miniature iron cells gasping for air, panting from exhaustion as the punishing heat turned the bosta into a large oven. When the door was finally opened and I was asked to step out of the truck, wearing my heavy shackles and with my hands and feet bleeding, I fainted. Everything went dark.

On that day, I was kept in that metal monstrosity for 14 hours, starting at five in the morning. The journey from the Ramleh Prison to the Jerusalem court should not require such arduous and long travel. But that is the whole point of the bosta truck. It is not like any other form of transport. It is meant to humiliate you, to torture you, to shatter your will. Once we arrived at the courthouse, the truck—which is divided into several tiny metal compartments, each barely enough for a single prisoner to sit down—would simply stand still. While we waited, the engine would rev for hours, exuding foul smells that polluted whatever little air we could breathe through the metal-barred windows.

On that day, I collapsed, despite my efforts to withhold any satisfaction my jailers would have from seeing me on my knees. My body was at its breaking point.

I was transported to a court in Jerusalem nine times during my last stay in prison, which lasted for 23 days. It was not my first arrest, nor will it be my last. My fight for the freedom of my people, for my Al-Aqsa Mosque and for my beautiful city of Al-Quds will not cease, prison or no prison, bosta or no bosta. Each day in their custody represents the same struggle: my Israeli jailers trying to break me, and my Jerusalemite pride, always fighting back.

On the first day of my arrival to prison, the guards stripped me completely naked. They searched me in ways so degrading, I cannot get myself to even write them down. All I can say is that they intentionally tried to deprive me of the slightest degree of human dignity. This practice, of stripping and of degrading body searches, would be repeated every time I was taken out of my cell and brought back.

Every day, the guards entered the cell for the routine body count. They would order me, along with other prisoners, to extend my arms outside the little trapdoor. They would then handcuff me before entering my cell. To be taken to interrogation, or to appear before court, they would chain my hands and feet together and drag me like an animal being taken to the slaughterhouse. That is when the bosta experience would commence. Imagine being shackled for over twelve hours a day, no food, no water and little air, crammed into a little metal box, your back pressed against a blistering metal wall, and your knees pushed against the opposite side—and all of this for simply defending the sanctity of my Mosque and the dignity of my city.

One time, as I was leaving the bosta truck, I tripped over my heavy shackles and fell. My feet were numb from sitting down in the same position for too many hours. As I fell, I barely touched the boot of a female solider. She claimed that I did that on purpose and that I was attempting to attack her. So she began hitting me, aided by other soldiers. "Take that, 'steadfast woman'!" the female soldiers yelled, as they all piled on top of me, mocking and punching.

I am not a stranger to Israeli prisons. I have been detained many times, interrogated, beaten, shackled and abused in every way. This time, however, I wanted to be stronger. "No crying this time around," I told myself, when they threw me into my cell. It was a two-by-two-meter room and was filled with dead cockroaches, and a leaking toilet that was covered in human excrement. The prison would be in total chaos: prisoners screaming in pain, prison guards shouting obscenities, loud noises all around me. But I would sit calmly and pray, read the Holy Quran and make supplications to God to protect my family and grant me freedom.

But then, following the fifth appearance in court, a prison guard told me that I would not be allowed to use my religious garb or my hijab head cover any more. Even then, I did not beg or cry. I cannot give them this much power over me. I would only weep quietly when they left me alone. No strange men have ever seen my uncovered body since I was a child. I have worn my hijab with pride all my life. Yet, here I was, at 40, exposed to strange men, whose main job was to torment and demean me. All I could do was pray without being covered, while beseeching God to forgive me. Whenever the soldiers entered my cell, I would sit in the corner and cover my face and wait for them to leave.

At one point, I could no longer withstand this, so I decided to resist with my voice. I shouted as loud as I could for hours: "O Muslims!" I cried, "O God, O my people, come to my rescue!" The guards shouted back with awful insults, but I did not stop. They threatened to kill me, but I did not stop. Finally, the prison administrator came and I told him that they could shackle me to the wall if they wished, but I would fight them back with my voice and I would not relent until I had my clothes back. That night, I finally prayed with my garb and scarf on. Without my cover, I felt that my skin was peeled off. My modesty is part of who I am. The Israelis may have the power to deprive me of my family and my freedom, but they will never succeed in taking my identity away from me.

The hardest part in all of this was seeing my children in court for the first time. I smiled at them and tried to tell them that they are forever in my heart, but the soldiers shouted and ordered me to be quiet. When my son yelled across the room: "God is with you, Mom!" they pounced on him, hitting and shouting. I could do nothing but scream: "Allahu Akbar!," because God is greater than them, their chains, their prisons, their phony courts, their bosta trucks and their injustice.

I am now back on the frontlines, despite all the risks. Al-Quds is too dear to me to quit, no matter the price.

Jerusalem is my home.

— Khadija Ahmad Ibrahim Khweis

19

LAST WORDS

Fouad Qasim al-Razim

FOUAD Qasim al-Razim was born in Al-Quds (Jerusalem) on December 9, 1957. He is the fourth of 17 brothers and sisters. He received his education in the city and in 1979, he earned a degree in Islamic Law from the Shari'a Institute of Al-Quds.

Al-Razim was detained by Israeli occupation forces on January 30, 1981 and was accused of killing an Israeli soldier. He was sentenced to three consecutive terms of life in prison, totaling 297 years. Al-Razim spent over 30 years in prison before he was released in a prisoner exchange between the Palestinian resistance and Israel on October 18, 2011. His long stay in prison earned him the title of "the Dean of Jerusalemite prisoners."

However, al-Razim's freedom was not complete, as he was released from a small cell to the large, open-air prison that is the Gaza Strip. Gaza has subsisted under a hermetic Israeli siege and has endured several destructive wars since 2006.

To ensure his children do not lose their legal rights and connection to Al-Quds, al-Razim married a Palestinian woman from Jenin, in the West Bank. This arrangement allowed his two children: his daughter, Mariam, five, and his son, Qasim, two, to visit the occupied Palestinian city, accompanied by their mother. The keenness in maintaining the Jerusalem connection, even if through his children, reflects Fouad's deep connection with the ancient Palestinian city, in which his family sank roots hundreds of years ago.

MY MOTHER WAS BROUGHT IN TO VISIT ME IN PRISON for the last time while on her hospital bed. She was barely conscious, wheeled in by a nurse and the ambulance driver into a small room located in the basement of Askalan Prison. I sensed that it was not an ordinary visit. Indeed, it was time to say my final goodbye.

The room in which she was allowed to meet me had no windows and no ventilation. It was a very hot, suffocating August day. The nurse and the driver left my mother in the company of my sister, Um Nidal, as they rushed outside to be in the fresh air. By the time I arrived after a long delay caused by strict prison security procedures, my mom was drowning in her sweat.

I have never seen her in such a distressing condition. Whenever I think of her, she is always on her feet, always strong and energetic. But on that day, August 24, 2005, her body was as thin as a skeleton. Medical tubes came out of her nose, while the veins of her arms had turned blue from the I.V. needles. It was the most difficult moment I had experienced throughout my 30 years in prison: my mother was on her deathbed, and I was in my shackles, unable to fully embrace her or feel her warm touch. I just lay my head on my sister's shoulder and cried.

The duration of the visit was merely 45 minutes. I spent them holding her hands, kissing her forehead, her feet, asking her to forgive me for any pain I had caused her from the day I was born up to that moment.

The arrangement, negotiated on my behalf by the Red Cross with the prison administration, permitted me to take three photographs with her. But the prison's Israeli photographer wanted to violate the agreement, insisting that we take only two photographs. I told them that they could not renege on the number of photos. I knew that their intention was simply to deprive me even of that symbolic right. I argued and quarreled with the guards and the photographer. Finally, they relented, but only when the matter was taken up to the head of the prison's administration.

At one point during the visit, the head of the prison—a vile, heartless man—and other top Israeli army officers stood nearby and just stared at us. I could see that gratified look on their faces, subtle smiles indicating that they were enjoying the scene of me sobbing by the side of my dying mother. A few minutes later, they turned around and walked away without saying a word.

I knew this would be the last time I would see Mom, so I urged her to repeat the Shahada after me: "There is No God but Allah and Muhammad is His Prophet."[72] She did not respond during the first few attempts but, in the end, I could see her lips moving, although her voice remained inaudible. I felt that she was spiritually ready for the final departure. The nurse and ambulance driver returned at the precise end of the visit and unsympathetically began pushing my mother's hospital bed outside the room. Um Nidal looked at me and said: "Please stay strong, brother; we draw our strength from you." I told her: "I will stay strong, if only for her sake."

Two prison guards grabbed both my arms and hurried me towards the door, on the way back to my cell. But as soon as my mother's bed was wheeled outside the room, I felt a

---

72 The Shahada is the Muslim profession of faith. Muslims consider reciting the Shahada to be the first of the Five Pillars of Islam.

strong emotional tug. I felt that I missed her so much, like never before, so I freed my arms from the Israeli officers and rushed outside the door, shouting her name, kissing her face and hands. For a brief moment, I felt truly liberated. Just when I came to accept the fact that I would never hear her voice again, she uttered, "May Allah bless you, Fouaz." She called me by my nickname, one that she had given me when I was still a child.

Exactly 20 days after that visit, as I sat with my comrades on the floor, ready to eat our dinner, a comrade yelled my name with much excitement. "Come and listen to the radio," he said, "Your family is sending you a greeting through the Palestine Radio Channel." I felt worried. My family came to see me once every two weeks, as they had done for many years. Why the radio greeting now? He turned the volume all the way up. My sister, Um Nidal, and my uncle's wife were on the radio. Their voices were filled with sadness. I immediately knew that my mother had died.

"Your mother is with God now, Fouad," my sister said. "She died while repeating your name until her last breath. She died pleased with you, brother."

Sudden gloom replaced the initial anticipation. I insisted that my comrades must sit down and eat their dinner. But we all sat down and stared at the floor and said nothing. At midnight, all my comrades went to sleep. I stayed up all night, lay my head down on the pillow and cried silently. I remembered all the good times, when the family was still all together, when we competed for my mother's attention. I thought of her smile and warmth and prayed to God that He may accept her soul into Paradise.

The next day, Ibrahim Meshaal, the brother who represents our demands to the prison administration, requested that we be allowed to hold funeral rites inside the prison courtyard during the foura. The administration refused, but we were not going to take no for an answer; we held the funeral rites in defiance of the prison, its administration and the prison guards. We prepared and smuggled the bitter coffee into the yard and served it to the mourners, fellow prisoners with whom I have shared my joys and pain for many years. They all hugged and kissed me. All the factions were there: Fatah, Hamas, the Socialists and the Communists. We, Palestinians, are always united by hardship.

My mother has left this world, but she still lives in my heart. I know that soon we will be together again.

—Fouad Qasim al-Razim

20

I long for my mother's bread My mother's coffee
    Her touch
Childhood memories grow up in me Day after day
I must be worth my life At the hour of my death
    Worth the tears of my mother.
And if I come back one day Take me as a veil to your
    eyelashes Cover my bones with the grass
Blessed by your footsteps Bind us together
    With a lock of your hair With a thread that trails from
    the back of your dress
I might become immortal Become a God If I touch the
    depths of your heart.
If I come back Use me as wood to feed your fire
    As the clothesline on the roof of your house
Without your blessing I am too weak to stand.
I am old Give me back the star maps of childhood
    So that I Along with the swallows Can chart the path
    Back to your waiting nest.

                                    —Mahmoud Darwish

MIRACULOUS BIRTH

Rafat Salah Mi'rif
—narrated by his mother, Farida Mahmoud Mi'rif

RAFAT Salah Mi'rif 'al-Qarawi' was born in Ramallah on December 19, 1982 to a poor family. He was the second eldest among four brothers and one sister. He went to school in the town of Beitunia. Due to the limited income of his family, Rafat, along with his brothers, did various kinds of labor, mostly in local farms—gathering watermelons and tomatoes and hauling boxes into trucks. He was only 13 years old when he began working.

The Mi'rif family first lived in the town of Ain Kenya, near Ramallah, before settling in Beitunia, located between Ramallah and Jerusalem. His father, Rashid, worked as a taxi driver. He passed away in 2012, at the age of 52. His mother, Farida, 58, works in the international relations office of the Palestinian Legislative Council (PLC) in Ramallah.

Rafat joined the First Intifada of 1987 when he was merely 8 years old, throwing stones at Israeli occupation soldiers who had repeatedly invaded his town, killing and wounding many of his peers and neighbors. He joined the Second Intifada of 2000, this time taking part in the armed struggle against Israeli forces. He was arrested on March 1, 2006, in al-Muqata'a, the Palestinian Authority government compound in Ramallah, together with the leader of the

Popular Front for the Liberation of Palestine, Ahmad Sa'dat, and others.

Rafat was tried in an Israeli military court and sentenced to 15 years in prison for his membership in the Al-Aqsa Martyrs Brigades, the military wing of the Fatah movement. He remains in prison to this day, serving a 16-year sentence in Askalan and Bir Al-Saba' prisons, respectively.

While in prison, Rafat enrolled in Al-Quds Open University, majoring in science.

———————

My son, Rafat, is fearless. His hard life taught him to be this way. He was thrown into the world of adults to fend for himself at a very young age. We had no other option. Our poverty was crushing. We were barely surviving.

I remember the day a large number of armed Israeli troops came chasing after Rafat during the First Intifada. He was not even 8 years old. He had thrown a stone at them, they claimed. Rafat had escaped their abuse by mere seconds. He ran through the main door of the house and out through the back door. The soldiers searched for him everywhere. They turned the house upside down, but could not find him. If my son had any fear in his heart, on that day it disappeared.

He joined the Second Intifada at 18. He was loved by everyone, always polite and considerate but always ready to defend the neighborhood whenever the Israelis invaded. The Israeli army kept trying to find and arrest him for six years after that, to no avail. After each raid, I would go out looking everywhere for him, not knowing if he was dead or alive.

In 2004, he married Mira, a beautiful girl from our village, who could neither talk nor hear. They grew up together in the same neighborhood. He was always protective of her. They were meant for each other, since birth. When he was arrested in 2006, they had no children. We were all worried that, by the time he would be released, Mira would not be able to have children any more.

In 2012, rumors were confirmed that a prisoner, Ammar al-Zubn, who was sentenced to hundreds of years in an Israeli prison because of his role in the resistance, managed to impregnate his wife from behind bars. People were saying that he had smuggled his sperm somehow, which eventually led to the birth of a gorgeous baby boy, Muhanad. Since that day, many more children were born in this way. The Prisoners Club says at least 64 such children were born to imprisoned fathers from 2012 to 2019.

One of those children is Amer. He is my grandson. Amer is now 6 years old. He is my pride and the happiness that has evaded Mira since her husband was arrested. The very idea that this beautiful boy lives and breathes is our triumph against the Israeli prison and the prison guard.

We are a people that love our freedom, and Amer is like a beautiful bird that flapped its wings and came soaring at us, bringing life and hope to Beitunia.[73] Since his arrival, so much has changed for the better.

It is like an impossible dream that came true, but it was not easy. At the start, Mira rejected the idea entirely. She communicated to me that our conservative society would not accept the idea and that the baby might be shunned by everyone. But as we observed how our Palestinian community was reacting to the babies who were born in this way, we felt reassured. The children were seen as miracles, and Palestinians felt a deep sense of pride that they were able to break free, somehow, even if their bodies remained shackled.

---

73 Beitunia is a Palestinian city in the West Bank, 8.7 miles (14 kilometers) north of Jerusalem.

The idea was first brought to me by Rafat himself when I visited him in Bir Al-Saba'. He told me that he dreams of being a father, but if Mira would not be able to have children by the time he is free, he would rather remain fatherless than take another wife. It was then that I tried to sell the idea to the family, including Mira's. I told them there was no shame in that. On the contrary, it is a message of defiance and freedom that our community will surely embrace.

Smuggling the sperm, however, was not easy. But it happened. I cannot describe the moment when baby Amer came with his mom to visit his father in prison. I joined them on that happy journey. Amer was only 9 months old. He was wearing his little pajamas. Rafat held him, kissed him, then held him tight and cried for a long time. We all did. For once, in many years, they were tears of joy.

And here you have it. Amer is a troublemaker just like his dad, running all around the house, so happy and without a care in the world. He reminds us of Rafat at that age.

Since my son was detained, my health has deteriorated. Now, I suffer from high blood pressure and my heart is weak. It has been a long time since I visited Rafat in prison. My body can no longer bear the brunt of the long journey to see him. But I will see him soon. I am counting the days for my son to be free. I will be waiting for him, together with Mira and Amer. We will dress Amer up with the cutest outfit and will have him wear a black and white kufiyeh, the enduring symbol of our freedom.

—Farida Mahmoud Mi'rif

21

MOHAMMAD'S WATCH

Bilal Khaled al-Tammam

BILAL al-Tammam was born on October 29, 1980 in the occupied Palestinian city of Tulkarm in the West Bank. He is the sixth among ten brothers and sisters. Throughout his life, Bilal took part in many protests in his city, demanding an end to the Israeli occupation. At 14, he was wounded in the leg by a gas canister fired by the Israeli army.

Bilal joined Al-Aqsa Martyrs Brigades in 2000, soon after his younger brother, Mohammad, was killed by the Israeli army during the early protests of the Second Palestinian Uprising, known as the Al-Aqsa Intifada (2000-2005)[74].

Bilal's armed resistance had been mostly confined to defending Tulkarm during the Intifada, but he ventured further out during the invasion of major Palestinian towns by the Israeli army in the spring of 2002.

---

74 "On 28 September 2000, the then opposition leader, Ariel Sharon, heavily guarded by Israeli soldiers and policemen, walked into al-Aqsa mosque in Jerusalem. It was a move certain to provoke an angry reaction from the Muslim population, who hold the mosque to be the third holiest site in Islam. Fighting broke out between the Palestinians defending al-Aqsa and security forces guarding Sharon. Seven Palestinians were killed in the fighting and thus the second Intifada—Intifada al-Aqsa—was started." "The Second Intifada," *Al Jazeera,* December 4, 2003, <https://www.aljazeera.com/archive/2003/12/20084101554875168.html>.

Bilal was arrested on August 7, 2002 and was sentenced by an Israeli military court to 30 years in prison for his role in the Intifada, for resisting the Israeli army and for his involvement with a militant group.

He remains in an Israeli prison to this day.

I WAS ONLY 14 when the Israeli Jewish terrorist, Baruch Goldstein, carried out the mass murder of many Palestinian worshippers in the Ibrahimi Mosque in Al-Khalil [Hebron] in February 1994. I remember marching in the streets of Tulkarm with my peers, denouncing the occupation and vowing to carry on with the legacy of the martyrs. All of Palestine rallied in solidarity with Al-Khalil during that time and many protesters were killed and wounded by Israeli soldiers.

I remember people running for cover as the soldiers arrived, showering us with many teargas canisters. One of these canisters hit my right knee with full force. It left a mark that is still visible after all these years.

This was only one episode that contributed to the eventual igniting of the Al-Aqsa Intifada in 2000. The uprising was instigated by Ariel Sharon[75] who raided the Al-Aqsa Mosque with hundreds of soldiers in September of that year, but it was not just a single event that caused our popular mobilization. When I learned that an uprising was building momentum, I left my job as a construction worker in Nazareth and hurried back to Tulkarm to take part in the protests.[76]

---

75 Ariel Sharon was an Israeli general and politician. He served as the country's minister of defense between 1981 and 1983 and the 11th prime minister from 2001 to 2006.

76 Nazareth is an Arab-majority city in the northern Galilee region. Tulkarm is a Palestinian city in the northwest of the occupied West Bank.

I will never forget that day, October 6, 2000. Tulkarm was swamped with protests and clashes between stone-throwing youth and the Israeli army. However, on that day, I was too tired to take part in the protest. I told my younger brother, Mohammad, to walk home with me. It was his birthday and I had bought a present for him. He had turned 19, and I felt that he deserved a good quality watch, for he was a handsome and much-loved young man. Alas, he refused, insisting that he would rather stay with the people in the street. He asked me to give him the watch later that evening.

I kept looking at the watch I bought him. It was a fancy watch. I could not wait for him to see it. It was getting late and Mohammad was still outside. Then, a friend phoned me.

"Your brother was shot and has been taken to hospital," he said.

He was a good friend, and we had often pulled heavy pranks on each other. So, a part of me did not believe him. But I could not dismiss the news entirely, and I decided to walk to the nearby hospital without telling anyone in the family. When I arrived there, people were particularly kind to me and some began hugging me and crying. Not only was my brother wounded, but also dead.

I later learned that Mohammad was shot by a sniper, as he stood at a distance away from the clashes. The bullet was meant to kill him, and it did. As I stared at Mohammad's watch after we buried him, I kept thinking to myself that I would avenge my brother, no matter the cost. The crimes of the occupation are no longer crimes against my community— in our streets, hospitals, at military checkpoints or random items in the news. These crimes have now entered through my family door and taken my young brother away from me. Mohammad and I were just like one person; we were like shadows of one another.

No, stones and slingshots to counter heavily armed soldiers will no longer suffice, I thought to myself. To avenge Mohammad, I needed more than such meaningless tools, so I joined Al-Aqsa Martyrs Brigades, the military arm of the Fatah movement. I was officially part of the armed struggle against the Israeli occupation.

A few months later, we learned that a massive Israeli army raid on the adjacent Tulkarm refugee camp had begun. I took my rifle and went running with the other young men to repel the attack, which involved massive army tanks. I began by immediately throwing a hand grenade at one of the tanks, hoping to halt the progress of the army, but it did not explode. I drew closer to the tank to investigate what had happened, only to be shot in the left leg by an Israeli sniper stationed on top of a nearby high building.

I remained on the ground and was saved by one of the girls in our camp. She bravely opened the door to her house and pulled me in. An ambulance soon arrived at the back of her house. They carried me to the hospital. After I was discharged, I walked on crutches for four months.

I did not return fully to the armed struggle until January 14, 2002. That was the day that my childhood friend, Raed al-Karmi,[77] was martyred. He was my dearest friend and a heroic figure for his daring resistance to the occupation. I did not want what happened to Mohammad and Raed to happen to others, so I picked up arms again. Eight months later, I was captured.

The Israeli army had lifted a long military curfew that it had imposed on the camp. It was a ploy. Lifting the curfew

---

77 Raed al-Karmi was the leader of an unofficial armed group within Fatah, known as the al-Aqsa Martyrs Brigades. He was assassinated by Israeli forces on January 14, 2002, at the age of 28. "Militants Avenge Israeli Killing," *The Guardian,* January 15, 2002, <https://www.theguardian.com/world/2002/jan/15/israel>.

meant that the army had retreated to the outskirts of the city. But not on that day. I was home with my friend, Ziad Da'as, who was also wanted by the Israeli army. All of a sudden, we realized that our house was surrounded from all directions and that Apache helicopters were circling overhead. Snipers were everywhere. The noise was deafening, as it was mixed with the barks of angry dogs. We scattered, confused, without a plan and fully trapped.

We both rushed to the roof. We needed to leave the house before the Israelis shelled it with my whole family inside. Ziad wanted to jump into a small garden at the back of the house. The garden was secluded, positioned in such a way that made it almost invisible to anyone, unless you see it from the roof of my house. In fact, jumping into the garden and zigzagging through the small alleyways was our agreed escape plan, in case the house was ever raided. But the moment Ziad peered his head over a small wall that encircled the roof, a bullet came flying, barely missing his head.

I urged him to just wait a moment and not raise his head. He replied, "Don't worry. Just give me a few seconds and I will figure something out." He peered over the wall one more time, only for a second, before a bullet penetrated his head. His upper half fell on the small wall, exposing it to Israeli army snipers who fired mercilessly. The bullets flew everywhere and I felt completely paralyzed, unable to help Ziad in any way or to simply pull his body towards me.

Confusion, combined with shock, numbed me. I retreated into the house to find the family all huddled together. My parents were holding on to my little sister, my brother, and my niece. "What is happening?" yelled my dad, with so much panic and fear in his eyes. I told them that Ziad had been killed. My mom began to weep, but her cries were quickly drowned by the army's loudspeakers, demanding that we give ourselves up.

I walked very slowly outside, with my arms behind my head. Israeli soldiers ordered me to lift my shirt up to show that I carried no weapons. I did. They ordered me to walk slowly towards them. When I arrived, they pushed me to the ground, handcuffed and blindfolded me. Only after they brought my father to identify me, did they know I was Bilal Tammam. One of the officers asked me about my comrade, Ziad. I told him that he was martyred. The officer laughed out loud and said mockingly in Arabic: "May Allah bless his soul."

Then they all started to beat me up, punching and kicking me while I was unable to defend myself.

"Say goodbye to your neighborhood," one officer said, "because we will make sure that you will never see it again."

I was not the only one of my family who was arrested. Hossam, too, was detained and sentenced to four years in prison. I was sentenced to 30 years. With Hossam and I in prison, my father's health deteriorated. He was still mourning the loss of Mohammad and was consumed by grief and stress. On August 15, 2004, my dad suffered a stroke and died.

It is one thing to endure hardship, injury, torture and imprisonment for decisions that you have made while fully aware of the consequences. But being in prison while learning about the tragedies that hit my family, one after the other, was just too much to bear. Two years after my father's death, my brother, Izz al-Din died in a car accident. I learned about it through the local Salam Radio station. "Izz al-Din Tammam died in a car accident earlier today," the news broadcast said, in a matter of fact way. My world came to a standstill. Izz al-Din was three years younger than me, and for four years, he had tried to visit me, but failed. The Israeli military denied his application numerous times, and he died without me hugging him or kissing his forehead.

Less than a year later, my sister, Iman, 28, died of a stroke, leaving behind four children. The news was relayed to me through my comrades in prison. A comrade said, "Sit down, Bilal, I need to tell you something." I immediately knew that another terrible thing had just happened to my family. He asked me if I was related to Umm Mohammad Tammam. They wanted to break the bad news gently but, considering all the tragedies in my life at that point, I could only assume the worst. "She is dead, isn't she?" I said, without a moment of hesitation, and to their surprise. Once that was confirmed, all I could do was lower my head and just cry, as I cried many times for my Dad, Izz al-Din, Mohammad, Raed, Ziad and all the people I have known, loved and lost.

I felt that my body and my mind had grown numb to misery. Crises were hitting me like electric shocks. I endured one, then got shocked again, and again. And there was no one that could help me through my pain, aside from my comrades in prison, who I felt I had burdened with my endless troubles while they had their own problems to deal with.

For the first ten years of my imprisonment, I was denied family visitations. Several members of my family died without my being able to see them at least once. When my mother and sisters were finally allowed to see me for the first time after this long isolation, I could hardly talk. I just cried as I felt that my father, Iman and Izz al-Din should have been there with me. My mother's eyes desperately held back tears. I felt that, in a few minutes, her eyes communicated to me the pain of a lifetime. I wanted to look into her eyes forever, and to throw myself at her so that she may hug me and make up for all the lost time I spent away from her. But the Israeli prison guard came and dragged me back to my cell.

I shared my cell with Fadi al-Dirbi, a gentle comrade who was also imprisoned for resisting the occupation. We began our relationship as prisoners sharing a room in the Ramon Prison. But we quickly became friends, even brothers, inseparable and always seeking strength in each other's company. On October 14, 2015, he died. He was ill, and we had petitioned the Israeli prison administration many times to allow him to see a doctor, but they refused. We were playing cards and chatting about all sorts of things, when he suddenly fell backward. He fainted and no one would come to his rescue, despite my pleas and shouts that my friend was dying. I held a funeral in my cell, where other prisoners—when they were allowed to leave their rooms—came to pay their respects. I held many funerals for loved ones since I came here.

Whenever life overwhelms me and I feel pain in my chest, I try to cope by writing how I feel on pieces of paper, which I then throw into the bin. I read somewhere that this is a good way to cope with hardship. Sometimes, I think that this might all be just a bad dream. That my father, brother and sister are all still alive and are waiting for me to return home. That time has stood still and that I will leave this place and be united with my loved ones, all of them. And, sometimes, I feel that Mohammad is still alive and, one day, I will get the chance to give him his gift, a fancy watch I bought for him nearly 20 years ago.

But time here keeps ticking slowly, and I just keep walking up and down, alone in my cell.

—Bilal Khaled al-Tammam

22

"NO PAIN LIKE MINE"

Israa' Riyad Ja'abis
—Narrated by her sister, Mona Ja'abis

ISRAA' Ja'abis was born on July 22, 1984 in Al-Quds (Jerusalem), the fourth of nine sisters and brothers. She was arrested following an electrical system failure in her car which caught fire while she was still trapped inside. It resulted in first, second and third degree burns on her face and all over her body, including the loss of eight fingers.

On the day of the accident, October 11, 2015, Israa' drove from Jericho to Al-Quds in a small car that was overflowing with household items. She was moving to Jerusalem with her son, Mu'tasim, and, by transporting some of the small furniture, she had hoped to save on moving expenses.

Israa' was moving to Jerusalem without her husband. Her only son, Mu'tasim, was born in Jerusalem and that qualified him for residence in the occupied city. She was allowed to stay with him as she, too, was a Jerusalem resident. His father, however, was barred from the city due to his West Bank ID card. The family agreed to separate for a number of years so that Mu'tasim would have the opportunity for better schooling and health care. Neither parent was thrilled by the decision, but they felt that they had no other option.

*One of the items that Israa' carried with her was a
propane tank for the kitchen. It would have been too expensive
to buy a brand new one in Jerusalem. As she was leaving
Jericho, the engine of her car died twice. Young people in
the town warned her to turn around and find another form of
transportation, but she did not heed their advice. She needed
to get to Jerusalem to her new job at a nursing home. Each
time her car died, the engine emitted a burning smell.*

*After travelling a couple of kilometers outside the
Israeli Al-Za'ayem military checkpoint, near the illegal
Jewish settlement of Ma'ale Adumim*[78] *and a short distance
east of Al-Quds, Israa's car died again. No soldiers or army
vehicles were in sight. A while later, a retired Israeli police
officer passed by her stalled car. He parked his car in front
of hers and asked for her ID as she desperately tried to
restart the car. "There is a strong smell in the car," she told
him, trying to exit the car, but he insisted that she stay inside
while he examined her papers.*

*She tried to open the windows, but they, too, were
affected by the electrical failure. Again, she tried to exit
the car, opening the door, but the officer rushed over and
slammed it shut, crushing her hand. She yelled "Allahu
Akbar 'alaiku" (God is greater than you are), chastising
him several times for not allowing her to escape. She urged
him to let her out as fire ignited in the front part of the car.
He refused. He stood there, watching her burn inside. The
airbag deployed, completely trapping her inside the blazing
car.*

*The police officer who stopped her claimed that she
was trying to use the propane tank to blow up the car. His
testimony was the only one considered in the Israeli court,*

---

78 Ma'ale Adumim is an illegal Jewish settlement 4.3 miles (7 kilometers)
east of Jerusalem.

and Israa' was branded a "terrorist." She was sentenced to 11 years in prison. She is now serving her term at HaSharon prison inside Israel, and is denied much-needed medical attention. After her debilitating injuries and imprisonment, her husband also suffered a car accident, leaving him permanently disabled and confined to a wheelchair. Their son, Mu'tasim, is now living with his grandmother in Jerusalem.

Mona is Israa's older sister and "best friend."

———————◆———————

IT IS TOO DIFFICULT TO DESCRIBE the first time we saw Israa'. We learned bits of information here and there about the nature of her wounds, and of the fact that some of her fingers were amputated. I thought that I was mentally prepared to see my sister in that condition, but I was wrong.

I visited her for the first time one week after the accident. I wore the attire of a religious Jewish woman to disguise myself in the hospital. I speak fluent Hebrew, and my dress and language skills allowed me access into the hospital. I made my way to the emergency ward and watched Israa' through a large glass window. There was a police officer sitting beside her, as if she could possibly move, let alone escape in that condition. I did not recognize her right away. Her face and body were bandaged and bloated. But I then recognized her through her height and her hair. The officer noticed my presence. I told him that I had lost my way, but he ordered me to leave.

I told my parents, who were waiting outside, that I saw her and that she was okay. I could not bring myself to tell them the truth.

Two months later, I returned with my parents. We were only permitted to see her from behind the glass window and were not allowed to talk to her. I will never forget the look on my parents' faces. Tears gushed from my father's eyes. He struggled to find words, but could not speak. My mother kept mumbling to herself, as if a mantra: "She is fine; she is fine; medicine will fix everything; she is fine…" Israa' was not aware of our presence. A group of Israeli officers were surrounding and interrogating her.

I was trying to prepare my nephew, Mu'tasim, for the transformation that had taken place. I told him that his mom had had an accident and that he would be allowed to meet her soon. But he is a smart kid. Although only eight years old at the time, he searched the news and found out what had happened. But he still could not find pictures of her after the accident. I sat with him again and told him: "I love my mother no matter what she looks like, white, black or red; whether her face is blemished or not." He said: "I love my mom, too, no matter what." Then I showed him a photo of her that was intentionally distorted. I did not want him to actually see right away how horrific her disfigurement was. He sat in silence for a long time. He seemed emotionally disconnected, as if the story was about someone else.

Israa' stayed in the hospital for three months. We were not even informed of her medical condition or progress. We would sneak into the hospital like thieves and, when the police discovered us, they would immediately throw us out.

The first time we were officially allowed to meet with her was in HaSharon prison. We were separated by a thick wall of glass. My mother only recognized her from her height, as Israa' is particularly tall. My mother rested her head in her hands and said nothing; she only wept.

I kept myself from crying, though. I told Israa': "We love you and we will stand by your side, no matter what the obstacles." My father seemed to have lost his mind. He hobbled around the room, crying: "Israa,' sweetheart. Israa,'

I am your father." Israa' kept telling him: "I am Israa,' Daddy. Please look, just look at me. My face is burned, but my heart, my mind and my whole being is still the same." I kept assuring him that this was Israa' but he was too confused and kept walking in circles, screaming her name. She was always a source of strength for him. When he finally realized that she was his daughter, he broke down, weeping like a child.

Israa' was the backbone of our family. When I visited her the second time, I told her: "You don't always have to be the strong one. It's okay to be vulnerable sometimes." As soon as I said that, she began crying, and she cried for a long time.

When Mu'tasim came with us to visit her for the first time, the prison administration did not allow him to enter. So I sat with him in the parking lot, waiting for my parents to come out. When they did, they were holding hands, wailing like little children. I went running towards them. They told me that they had amputated all of her fingers except two. Then we praised Allah for allowing her to keep the two fingers.

A year and two months later, Mu'tasim was finally allowed to see her. He was nine years old then. I took him, as my mother could no longer cope with the pain of seeing her daughter in that condition. But the prison guards did not allow me access to her room. They only allowed Mu'tasim to talk to her from behind the glass barrier. He begged them to let him hug his mother and, finally, they relented, agreeing to allow him to spend ten minutes with her. I watched from behind the glass as Israa' walked in wearing a Tigger costume. She had sewn it inside the prison, as she knows how much Mu'tasim loves the Winnie the Pooh cartoon. She even designed and wore a Tigger mask. When Israa' was younger, she loved to dress up in costumes and perform as a clown for various community events for children. Mu'tasim told her: "I know you are my mother. I don't want Tigger. I want to see your face." So she removed the mask. Mu'tasim was shocked. His eyes filled quickly with tears. He told her: "I love you, no matter what." He told her that the "acne on your face will soon go away." When it was time to leave, he clung to her, refusing to let go. The guards asked me to intervene. Mu'tasim kept repeating: "You either let me stay, or let her come home with me."

On the way home, Mu'tasim told me, after a long silence: "My mom will always be beautiful, even if the acne never goes away."

My heart breaks for Israa,' my tall, slender, sister with a beautiful face, the lovely one whose hands were always adorned with henna. In her we saw hope, strength and beauty. The harshness of the occupier scarred her face and body, amputated her fingers and is relentlessly trying to break her spirit. I will never forget when a journalist asked her across the court room, as she sat surrounded by armed Israeli officers: "Are you in pain?" She raised whatever remained of her hands and answered: "No pain is like mine."

If I could only take even some of my sister's pain away…

—*Mona Ja'abis*

23

"I SEE YOU IN MY HEART"

Faris Baroud
—Narrated by his mother, Ria Baroud

FARIS Baroud was arrested on March 23, 1991. An Israeli military court sentenced him to 134 years in prison, accusing him of killing an Israeli settler who was taking part in the military occupation of Gaza.

Ria, Faris' mother, was forbidden to visit her son in the Nafha Prison for the last 15 years. The 70-year-old mother was told that the decision was motivated by security concerns.

Faris was Ria's only son. He was born in 1968, two years after the start of the Israeli military occupation of Gaza. His father, Ahmad Mohammad Baroud, died when Faris was still a child. Ria, who remained unmarried after the death of her husband, dedicated her life to raising Faris. They lived together in a small home in the Shati' Refugee Camp in Gaza.[79]

Ria was only a teenager when her family was forced out of their village of Beit Daras in southern Palestine.

79 According to the United Nations Relief and Works Agency (UNRWA), "Beach Camp" is the third largest of the Gaza Strip's eight refugee camps and one of the most crowded. The Beach refugee camp is known locally as "Shati." The camp is on the Mediterranean coast in the Gaza City area. United Nations, accessed July 30, 2019, <https://www.unrwa.org/where-we-work/gaza-strip/beach-camp>.

Despite fierce resistance by the villagers, Beit Daras was conquered in May 1948. Hundreds of its people were killed and wounded, and thousands were expelled, mostly to Gaza. Beit Daras was entirely demolished soon after it was depopulated, and is now a part of the state of Israel.

Faris was reportedly tortured and held for nearly 10 years in solitary confinement. He was also denied family visitation for more than half of his time in prison. Prior to his arrest, he suffered from asthma, a condition that worsened with time.

Years after his imprisonment, Faris developed kidney disease, which worsened through medical negligence, further compounded by his participation in various hunger strikes in solidarity with other prisoners.

Time and again, Faris was denied early release, starting immediately after the signing of the Oslo Accords in 1993 and following a prisoner exchange in 2011. Along with 29 other prisoners, he was scheduled to be set free in 2013 or 2014, in a special arrangement that was also thwarted by the Israeli government.

Starting in 2002, Ria was denied visits with her son. Despite her deteriorating health and the gradual loss of her vision due to glaucoma, she was known for never missing a single vigil that was held regularly by families of Palestinian prisoners, in front of the Red Cross office, every Monday on Gaza City's famous Jala' Street.

At times, she would be the only one there, always holding the same framed picture of her son, Faris, close to her heart.[80]

---

80   The story of Ria Baroud was based mostly on her own narration published in Palestinian media. The bulk of her comments and the song were taken from a video interview conducted by Shehab News Agency. The full video interview can be found here: <https://www.facebook.com/watch/?v=517066045447053>.

I USED TO WAKE UP IN THE MORNING TO YOUR FACE, as your framed photo is always by the side of my mattress. But since I lost my sight, crying for you, son, I can only see you in my heart. I have so much faith that I will hold you in my arms again.

Not to worry, Faris, all thanks to Allah, I do everything on my own. I live alone, but I manage. I know where everything is and can reach everything in our house with ease. I still cook, but I no longer use the wood stove as I am scared of burning myself. So I use the gas stove. I no longer have the old one. It has been acting up, so I threw it away, and replaced it with a new one.

I try to do a lot of good deeds, son, because I believe that the more I give, the more God gives me back, by keeping you safe. I cook for myself and for the children in the neighborhood. My neighbor is a very old and poor woman. She does not have a gas stove, so I cook for her as well. All I ask in return is for people to say a prayer: "May Allah set your son free."

All I want in this life is to see you once before I die.

I called on all Arab and foreign countries, and all of Europe, and Jordan and Syria and the whole Arab nation to help me so that you can return to me. I told them through the news media that my son has been in prison since 1991, and I have not been allowed to visit him for the last 15 years. I hope they listen to a mother's pleas and help me.

When the Israelis told me that I am not allowed to see you, I cried until I turned blind, but I remember your handsome face exactly the way I saw you the last time we were together; it is an image that never leaves my mind.

When the prisoner exchange took place, I anticipated your release, so I bought a new bedroom set for you. It is always made up and ready. But you were not released, and I was still unable to see you. Maybe they were angry with me because of what happened the last time I came to visit you. I was climbing the stairs of the prison. It had more than 50 steps going up and 50 steps coming down. As I struggled on the ascent, I said to myself, "Oh, my son," as I was eager to see you. An Israeli soldier started to mock me. "Are you Hamas?" he said, laughing. I told him to shut up. "Do you see me carrying a weapon?" I yelled at him. When I returned the following time, the same soldier blocked my entrance. He said: "Go home, you no longer have visitation privileges."

It has been 15 years since I saw your face, but I have protested every week in front of the Red Cross office in Gaza, while holding your framed picture. And I thank Allah every day for you, son. Everyone who met you in prison, and is now free, came to visit me. They tell me that you are loved by everyone, and have such a good reputation. I tell them, and everyone else, that Faris is a hero. You are my hero.

Oh, how I cried for you, Faris. My eyes can only tell day from night, but nothing else. But thanks to God, thanks to God, I am content with my fate, for this is what Allah has decided for me. It is you that I am concerned about. So, I pray all day, every day. I make supplications to God so that you come back, and that I may choose your bride for you. We will throw a big party and all the neighbors and friends, all the Barouds and all the freed prisoners and their families will come and celebrate with us.

I also wrote a song for you and I sing it every time I hold my vigil in front of the Red Cross office:

They got out of jail and trashed its doors
I can't even breathe in here, yumma[81]
He can't breathe and he's torn away from his loved ones

---

81 "Yumma" is the colloquial Palestinian word for "Mom."

I swear I'd knock a jailer's teeth out

I'd break down the prison door for you, wallah with my hands

I'd knock it down.

Yes, I will break the door down. I am an old woman but my will comes from my love for you and from the help of God.

I leave you with this prayer, Faris,

"Oh, Allah, free my son and all of his comrades, all in one day, Amen. Oh, Allah, you are the one who grants victory and freedom, I beseech you to grant my son his freedom. Please set Faris and all the captive young men and women free.

"Oh, Allah, oh, Allah, oh Allah, give me back my son."

—*Ria Baroud*

RIA BAROUD died on May 18, 2017, at the age of 85. She spent nearly one third of her life waiting to see her son, Faris, free once more.

Soon after his mother's death, Faris' health took a turn for the worse. He developed an aggressive form of glaucoma as well, and had reportedly lost 80 percent of his vision.

Faris died on February 6, 2019 at the Nafha Prison in the Naqab Desert.

He was 51 years old.

Ria's last words were: "My only wish is to hold my son and kiss his forehead, just once before I die."

Both departed this life alone, blind, to never see each other again—at least in this life.

Dalia Al-Kayyali

WHY INTERNATIONAL LAW MATTERS TO PALESTINIAN PRISONERS, BUT NOT TO ISRAEL

Richard Falk

THE RELEVANCE of international law to the experience of Palestinian prisoners has always been problematic for several reasons. First and foremost, Israel has put forward its own legal narrative that attempts to marginalize international humanitarian law (IHL) as it applies to the Palestinian people. In Occupied Palestine, it treats Palestinians accused of criminal activity as not entitled to invoke prisoner of war status, but mere criminals subject to the law as administered by the Israeli military authorities. If pressed, Israel regards Palestinians accused of even minor and symbolic political crimes as "terrorists" and, thus, as having no acceptable legal claim to be treated as civilians protected under the Geneva Conventions. In a further Israeli innovation, Occupied Palestine is not treated as a legally relevant category, as East Jerusalem has been annexed, Israeli forces and settlers "disengaged" from Gaza in 2005, and the West Bank is "disputed sovereignty," lacking a legitimate sovereign authority, as well as being part of Israel's "promised land." From such a partisan legal perspective, Palestinian prisoners are deprived of their legal rights, and any protection given is an expression of Israeli generosity that derives not from any obligatory legal framework, but from self-proclaimed humanitarianism. Such an extra-legal claim by Israel should be dismissed as perverse, even ludicrous, in view of the consistent abusive arrest, trial, detention procedures and wretched prison conditions imposed on Palestinians that fall far below the prescriptions of international law.

This Israeli self-exemption from the discipline of international humanitarian law clashes directly with the international consensus that is virtually undivided when it comes to the application of IHL to Occupied Palestine. In more operational language, this means that the Fourth Geneva Convention of 1949 applies, as does customary international law applicable to belligerency and armed struggle, with respect to protecting those accused and convicted of crimes associated with resisting an unlawful occupation. From this perspective, Palestinians accused of crimes or subject to unlawful detention, and confined to Israeli prisons, are legally entitled to the full protection of international law, including applicable international human rights standards. Israeli unilateral justifications in the form of annexation, disengagement, and disputed sovereignty are legally irrelevant, or worse, despite being behaviorally relied upon to rationalize the inapplicability of international law to Palestinian prisoners. This legal assessment validates the authoritative international narrative that strongly upholds the applicability of IHL and invalidates the opposing Israeli legal rationalizations. The international narrative has been vindicated by a near unanimous set of findings by the International Court of Justice in its 2004 Advisory Opinion, calling for the dismantling of the Israeli separation wall.

In effect, IHL, properly interpreted and applied, is completely supportive of the grievances of Palestinian prisoners, but its applicability has been deliberately manipulated, the international consensus defied, and the prolonged abuse of Palestinian prisoner rights continued on a daily basis. Such a pattern of violation, without adverse consequences for Israel, makes it reasonable for Palestinians and their supporters to ask, of what use is international law if it is systematically violated and nothing happens in response? This question is particularly pertinent here, where Israel's defiance of its obligations under international law is so overt, and still no adverse consequences occur because these horrendous abuses of prisoner rights are shielded from international accountability by geopolitical muscle, which neuters the UN and human rights NGOs, making them incapable of implementing findings decisively supportive of Palestinian legally well-evidenced grievances.

Beyond these considerations are the commitments of Palestinians to the liberation of their country. Their acts of opposition to the Israeli presence, whatever form they take, are legally, politically, and morally empowered because of their being an integral part of a legitimate war of national liberation, a struggle against colonialist occupation rendered lawful by the General Assembly Resolution on Principles of International Law Governing Peaceful Co-Existence. In other words, Palestinian rights of resistance prevail over Israeli security and terrorist claims, at least so long as Palestinians themselves adhere to the International Law of War in carrying on their struggle. As the heart-rending statements of prisoners and their close relatives collected in this volume make vividly clear, their motivations are moral and political, with no expectations that Israelis will act in accord with relevant legal rules and principles. At the same time, in reaction to their experiences of abuse over so many decades, Palestinian prisoners have justified their sustained protest campaigns and hunger strikes against abusive prison conditions by invoking Israeli failures to live up to international human rights and IHL legal standards. In a few instances, Israel has actually retreated under these pressures from the prisoners, evidently seeking to avoid bad media publicity, by accepting some prisoner demands on such issues as medical treatment and family visits. Such victories for prisoner resistance underscore the earlier contention that international law can be made relevant if sufficient political traction for its implementation is brought to bear. Here, that traction comes not from the UN or governments or even an outraged international public opinion, but from the courage and desperate bravery of the prisoners themselves. It accords with the basic argument being made here, that minimal adherence to international law standards on Israeli prison conditions is more likely to be achieved by Palestinian resistance activity than by the United Nations or even the International Court of Justice. Such is this essential link between law and politics that Palestinians have learned the hard way, over the course of decades of disillusionment resulting from their legal rights being authoritatively affirmed, and still nothing happens by way of Israeli compliance.

Also relevant is the increasing acceptance in the political discourse of those who support the Palestinian national struggle that Israel maintains its control over Palestinians by reliance on apartheid structures. Such structures have been criminalized by the UN Convention on the Suppression and Punishment of the Crime of Apartheid (1973) and as a Crime Against Humanity in Article 7(j) of the Rome Statute governing the International Criminal Court. The allegation being made is that Israel's policies and practices, including its manner of administering criminal law and the conditions imposed on those detained and imprisoned, is thus a continuing crime of the greatest magnitude against the Palestine people as a whole. It further follows from the Apartheid Convention that the governments of the world are themselves derelict by failing to take steps to suppress and punish Israeli apartheid.

Given these realities, is it a waste of time for NGOs (such as Al Haq, Addameer, Btselem, Human Rights Watch, Amnesty International, and others) and international law scholars to document the grounds for concluding that Israel's treatment of Palestinian prisoners violates IHL and international human rights standards? How does it help these Palestinian prisoners who have been so often humiliated and victimized while being confined unjustly and unlawfully in Israeli prisons, if, arguably, their only tangible gains in treatment and conditions have resulted from their own acts of heroic self-reliance? Israel's dreadful record of torture and mistreatment of Palestinian prisoners, including women and children, has ironically coincided with Israel's greater diplomatic acceptance within its region and the wider world. Such a distressing observation confirms the view that it is a serious mistake to expect justice and lawfulness to be achieved by convincing governments and international institutions of Israel's defiant attitudes toward international law. Such defiance is widely acknowledged in government circles in the West, while at the same time steadfastly ignored, as other concerns take precedence in the formation of national policy. Fortunately, this cynical reality is not the end of the story.

The rationale for Palestinian resistance is heightened by having law and morality on the side of demands for an end to the oppressive Israeli occupation and the persistent abuse of fundamental Palestinian rights, with special attention to the inalienable right of all peoples to self-determination. It is this sense of national entitlement that mobilized mass discontent of captive national populations throughout the non-Western world that finally brought colonialism to an end. Additionally, Palestinian prospects for a just and peaceful future depend on supplementing resistance by a global solidarity movement. This movement of people on behalf of the Palestinian national struggle is strengthened by documenting Israeli violations of prisoner rights, under the auspices of the UN Human Rights Council and widely trusted NGOs, which also, to some extent, offsets Israeli hasbara that so often induces the most influential global media outlets to ignore or greatly minimize Israeli abuses of prisoner rights. Gaining transparency with respect to international law and morality helps to alter the balance of power in a struggle of national liberation. It has the indirect effect of strengthening support for such initiatives as the transnational BDS Campaign. This is the central explanation of the great victories of anti-colonial struggles in the last century, achieved in the face of the overwhelming military superiority of the colonial power. Israel has so far escaped this fate, but for how long?

As Ramzy Baroud so persuasively explains in his Introduction, these overarching structural crimes of Israel result in the imprisonment and subjugation of the entire Palestinian population, including even involuntary exiles who are denied a right of return to their homeland. In effect, those in Israeli prisons are metaphors of this wider condition, bearing witness to the pervasive injustice of treating specific acts of Palestinians as crimes that are more properly understood as legally authorized resistance to the systemic criminality of Israel, in the form of colonialism as reinforced by the distinct crime of apartheid. The extraordinary sacrifices, in some cases unto death, of Palestinian prisoners whose statements before our eyes convey so well the phenomenology of Israeli prison life, should not weaken our sense that colonial/apartheid oppression of the Palestinian people imposes prison conditions, and not just metaphorically, but in forms producing severe and sustained suffering. At its core, this represents a collective crime against an entire people who have been denied their most basic individual and collective rights for over seven decades, rights that are endorsed, and supposedly upheld, by international law.

—Richard Falk, former United Nations
Special Rapporteur on the Situation of
Human Rights in the Palestinian Territories

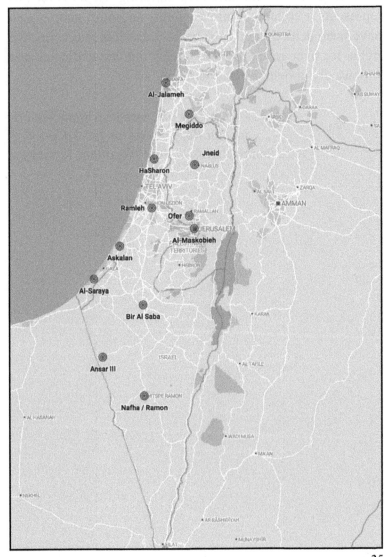

APPENDIX
ISRAELI PRISONS

AFOULEH HOSPITAL

Afouleh Hospital, located in the town of Afuleh (Afula), near Nazareth, is a civilian facility, but many Palestinian prisoners have been admitted there for treatment, especially during or following hunger strikes.

Palestinian prisoners in Afouleh are held under tight security and are often tied to their beds, even when on prolonged hunger strikes.

AL-JALAMEH (KISHON) PRISON

Al-Jalameh, or Al-Jalama is a high-security prison and interrogation center located between the cities of Haifa and Nazareth. It is officially known as Kishon prison.

AL-MASKOBIEH

Al-Maskobieh is an interrogation and investigation center located in West Jerusalem, where prisoners are held before being transferred to other prison facilities.

It is known for brutal interrogation tactics.

AL-SARAYA (GAZA CENTRAL PRISON)

Gaza Central Prison - also known as Al-Saraya - was located in Gaza City. It was used by several military administrations that ruled over Palestinians starting in the 1930s during the British Mandate over Palestine, then by Egypt, and finally, by Israel.

Following the Oslo Accords and the establishment of the Palestinian Authority (PA) in 1994, the prison was used to detain and often torture Palestinian political dissidents who opposed Oslo.

Al-Saraya was completely destroyed by Israeli F-16 fighter jets in the Israeli war on Gaza in 2008-9. Subsequently, it has been converted by Palestinians into a museum.

ANSAR III (KETZIOT) PRISON

Known by Palestinians as Ansar III and often referred to as the Naqab (Negev) prison, Ketziot prison is located in the Naqab desert.

Opened in 1988, Ansar III is divided into three large sections. According to the Palestinian prisoner support group, Addameer, "Section B consists of caravans or virtually mobile rooms," and prisoners are deliberately "left in the sun for long periods under the pretext of inspections."

ASKALAN (ASHKELON) PRISON

The Askalan prison is officially called the Shima prison but referred to as Askalan because it is located in the city of Ashkelon, 13 kilometers north of the fence separating the Gaza Strip from Israel.

The prison started receiving Palestinian prisoners in 1970. The prison facility includes a special wing where the notorious Israeli Security Services (Shabak) interrogate Palestinian and other Arab prisoners.

BIR AL SABA (OHALEI KEIDAR) PRISON

Ohalei Keidar prison complex is located in the town of Bir Al-Saba (Beersheba) in southern Israel.

According to Addameer, the complex is divided into four prisons: Ohalei Keidar and Eshel for security prisoners, Dekel for criminal prisoners, and Ayala, Israel's first private prison.

HASHARON PRISON

The HaSharon prison is located approximately 30 kilometers northeast of Tel Aviv.

HaSharon is particularly infamous for having two sections, one dedicated to incarcerating Palestinian children and another for women.

JNEID PRISON

Jneid prison is located in the Palestinian town of Nablus in the West Bank and is operated by the Palestinian Authority. Jneid is often used to detain Palestinian political dissidents who oppose the PA.

KHIAM PRISON

Khiam prison was a detention and interrogation camp located near the Lebanese town of Khiam. It was used during the years of Israeli occupation of south Lebanon, which ended in 2000.

MEGIDDO PRISON

The Megiddo prison is located approximately 35 kilometers southeast of Haifa.

The prison was used by Britain during its Mandate over Palestine, and was later utilized by the Israelis to detain Palestinians.

Megiddo prison holds Palestinian administrative detainees and children, and has a special section for isolating prisoners.

NAFHA & RAMON PRISONS

The Nafha and Ramon prisons share the same location deep in the Naqab desert, 200 kilometers south of Jerusalem.

Both are considered maximum-security prisons. While Nafha is based in an old structure, Ramon was recently built. Since 2006, Ramon prison has been used to detain "security prisoners," as it includes a special wing to keep Palestinians in complete isolation.

OFER PRISON

Ofer prison, also known as "Ofer Camp," was built on Palestinian land belonging to the West Bank village of Beitunia, near Ramallah.

Ofer Prison holds Palestinian child prisoners as well as administrative detainees.

RAMLEH (RAMLA) PRISON

The Ramleh prison is located in the city of Ramleh in central Israel. It was established in 1934 as the Ramleh Palace, to be later converted by Israel into a military base in 1953.

There are currently five prison facilities in Ramleh, including the maximum-security Ayalon prison and a women's prison, Neve Tirza.

SOURCES:

Addameer website
Al Jazeera English
Middle East Monitor
International Middle East Media Center (IMEMC)